You and the Computer

a course in computer literacy

Jo Lloyd and Chris West

Edward Arnold

© Jo Lloyd and Chris West 1984

First published in Great Britain 1984 by
Edward Arnold (Publishers) Ltd
41 Bedford Square
London
WC1B 3DQ

Edward Arnold (Australia) Pty Ltd
80 Waverley Road
Caulfield East
Victoria 3145
Australia

Reprinted 1984

British Library Cataloguing in Publication Data
Lloyd, Jo
   You and the computer.
   1. Electronic digital computers
   I. Title   II. Lloyd, Jo
   001.64   QA76.5

   ISBN 0-7131-0927-0

Text set in 11/13 Times Roman Compugraphic
by Colset Private Limited, Singapore
Printed and bound by Spottiswoode Ballantyne
Limited, Colchester and London

Contents

Foreword

This book gives a simple introduction to computers, particularly microcomputers, and their applications. It has been written to enable the reader to become computer literate, ie to be familiar with the nature and vocabulary of computers, to be able to operate a microcomputer, to appreciate the function of computer programs, to be aware of a wide range of applications for computing, and to recognize the social implications of the technology both now and in its future use.

The material in this book has been developed from the authors' experience of teaching computer literacy to a wide range of people, from vocational preparation students in Further Education to well-qualified adults with no computer experience. The book is aimed at anyone who has not had a formal computer education but wishes to find out about computers and relate them to the world of work, leisure or the home. It is intended to be used as a supporting textbook for Computer Literacy courses in Secondary Schools, Further Education and on the Youth Training Scheme where Computer Literacy is a compulsory core component. It can also be used as an introductory self-teaching text for interested adults. Computer Literacy courses will need to be supported by appropriate microcomputer resources such as those detailed in the Further Education Unit Report 'Computer Literacy', 1983, which was written by the authors of this book and their associates.

The book aims to make the reader computer literate by relating computers and their uses to experiences in everyday life. Each chapter links back to learning objectives which are given at the beginning. There are numerous exercises and 'things to do' which are independent of specific equipment. The book refers to well-known educational microcomputers to demonstrate various aspects of Computer Literacy.

Introduction

You may have noticed that you've been hearing and seeing a lot of information about computers recently. They're in the news. There are so many of them now, doing so many different jobs, that people are saying that we're in the middle of a 'computer revolution'.

What's happened is that over the years computers have become smaller, cheaper and more powerful. Because of this they're being used to do more and more things. Wherever you go in life, whatever work you do or would like to do, you're likely to run into a computer at some point. You'll find them in shops; many cash tills now contain small ones. In the office, they'll be helping to run the business, or perhaps you'll come across one being used as a sophisticated typewriter. In industry, they're to be found on the shop floor, controlling robots which help in the manufacture of goods. In the High Street, you may notice outside main banks, computer-controlled cash points which people can use to withdraw money from their current accounts. If you follow the sports news, the chances are that the results for your favourite sport are now produced by computer. Computer technology can even be found in the home, in ordinary domestic appliances such as cookers, radios and washing machines. In fact, small computers have become so cheap now that many people are buying their own simply to try them out and see what they can do.

So why do you need to learn anything about them? Well, since you're going to keep coming across them, you'll find it a great help if they're not just mysterious black boxes to you. You don't need a degree in computer science or a string of CSE's to your credit; no-one's going to ask you to start designing computers yourself, or expect you to become a programmer or an engineer. What will be useful, however, is if you can learn enough about computers to make the most of any that you come across in your daily life. Once you understand what a computer is, what it can and can't do, and how to make it work for you, you can sit back and relax, knowing that you're well equipped to handle the new technology. And who knows, you may even find that it helps you to get a job!

Acknowledgements

The publishers would like to thank the following for their permission to reproduce copyright illustrations:

Crown Copyright, The Science Museum, p. 46;
Crown Copyright, The Science Museum & The United States Army, p. 48b;
Crown Copyright, C.O.I., p. 100;
Sinclair Research Ltd, pp. 7 & 17
I.B.M.(U.K.) Ltd, pp. 11 (all), 13, 14br, 15, 16, 18b, 73t & 87;
H.J. Heintz Co. Ltd., p. 12t;
Gloucester College of Art & Technology, pp. 12b, 14tr & bl;
I.C.L. Ltd, pp. 14tl, 18t & 73b;
Acorn Computers, p. 21;
John Baguley, p. 42;
Ferranti plc, pp. 45, 48t & 50t;
Mullard Ltd, pp. 49, 52, 53, 54 & 55tab;
Phillips Electronics, p. 50b;
Rank Xerox (U.K.) Ltd, p. 57;
Farmers Weekly, p. 58t (Millington);
Micro Scope Ltd, p. 58c;
Chubb Alarms Ltd, p. 58b;
Diana Lanham, pp. 60, 64b;
Vivien Fifield Picture Library, p. 64t;
Ozalid (U.K.) Ltd, p. 65;
Anthony McAvoy, p. 66;
Burroughs Machines Ltd, p. 67;
Hewlett-Packard Ltd, p. 78;
British Airways, p. 81;
House of Commons Public Information Office, p. 83t;
CAP U.K. Ltd, p. 83b;
Thomas Cooke Ltd, p. 86;
Prestel, British Telecom, p. 89;
Powertran, p. 97;
Keith Butcher, p. 98;
Science Photo Library, p. 99;
Austin Rover Group Ltd, p. 103tab;

The authors would like to thank the following:
— The Further Education Unit, for supporting the work which led to the development of these ideas;
— Gloucestershire College of Art and Technology, for support, and for permission to use pictures of the computer facilities;
— Jim Taylor, without whom this book would not have been possible.

1

What is a computer?

What will this chapter teach you?
This chapter will introduce you to computers by describing them and telling you what they can do. As you work through it, you'll be doing the following:

1 meeting some of the special words used in computing and finding out what they mean;

2 looking at the way computers work by comparing them with your own body and its functions;

3 finding out about the different parts of a computer system, and looking at some common pieces of computer equipment;

4 learning to recognize different types of computer.

---

1 What is a computer?

Imagine that a creature from outer space has landed on Earth and come to meet you. During the long journey to reach our planet, the creature has been teaching itself English by listening to earth radio, and now speaks it quite well, apart from one problem: it has no idea what a computer is. Since it keeps hearing the word used, it is interested and asks you to explain it.

Could you give a clear, simple description of a computer? Perhaps your answer would be like one of these:

'Well, it's a sort of machine in a box. It can do things. . . .'

So can a sewing machine, or a typewriter; but they're not computers.

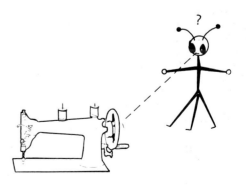

'It's a kind of brain. It's good at complicated sums.'

That sounds like the maths teacher.

'It's a machine that runs on electricity and does calculations.'

Better, but still not right. You could be describing one of the old-fashioned adding machines.

'It's an electronic machine for processing data automatically.'

Right!

But what does that *mean*? Let's look at each word in turn:

ELECTRONIC doesn't just mean that a computer is powered by electricity, although it is; an electronic machine is one that contains small but powerful parts such as *transistors* and *silicon chips* (see chapter 4). Radios and pocket calculators are examples of electronic devices.

DATA is what we feed into the computer. It can be facts, figures, instructions, words, sentences; anything at all that is used as input.

PROCESSING is what the computer does with the data which we have fed in. This doesn't just mean doing calculations on figures; that's only one part of a computer's job. Computers can also compare things with each other, handle text, fetch records, store information, sort things into order, answer questions, and move information from place to place. Jobs like this are all forms of processing and can be done by a computer without the need for human intervention; that is, automatically.

Things to do

1 List *three* electronic devices which you have used.
2 Consider whether a pocket calculator is a computer, and explain what you have decided and why.
3 Draw a simple diagram of a computer.

2 How does a computer work?

You and the computer

Have you ever tried to compare yourself with a computer? If not, do it now. Which do you think is the more intelligent, adaptable, complicated, expensive, difficult to replace?

The answer is, you. You win on every one of these counts. The computer hasn't yet been made that can even begin to challenge the human brain. People are in a completely different league from machines, no matter how sophisticated the machines are. Computers have a reputation for being extremely clever but, in fact, left to themselves they're rather stupid. A computer can only do exactly what it has been told to do by somebody; it isn't capable of thinking of anything by itself. Believe it or not, you're far brighter than the most expensive computer ever made!

But if this is the case, why are computers generally regarded as being very intelligent? Well, the one big advantage that a computer *does* have over you is that it's fast. When it's processing data, all that it's doing is following instructions which someone has given it, but it's following them at a far greater speed than you could. This is what makes computers so useful. Generally speaking, the bigger and more expensive the computer is, the more data it can handle and the faster it can process it. Because of this, a computer is ideal for any job that involves a great deal of repetitive work – for example, producing thousands of letters to be sent out together, or calculating the vast distances between the stars.

Let's compare you and a computer in more detail. This is useful because, although you are much more complicated than the computer, you work in a similar way. For every part of the computer, there's a part of you which performs roughly the same function, and so looking at the way you work will help us to understand the way in which the computer operates.

How do you work?

You are controlled by your brain. This receives information from various parts of your body. These parts can be thought of as *INPUT* devices.

One example of an input device is the ear, which receives information in the form of sound. Sound is then the *INPUT MEDIUM* – this means the form in which the input message comes.

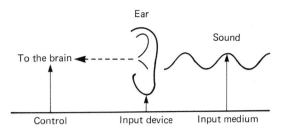

What other input devices do you have, and what medium do they use? This list has already been started for you; see if you can add to it, in your workbook.

	INPUT DEVICE	MEDIUM
1	Ear	Sound
2	Eye	Light

When the information which has been input arrives at the brain, it is processed and the brain makes a decision on what to do about it. Messages are then sent from the brain to other parts of the body, telling them what action to take. These actions are a form of *OUTPUT*, and the part of the body which is used for the action is an *OUTPUT DEVICE*.

One example of an output device is the mouth – sound is then the *OUTPUT MEDIUM*.

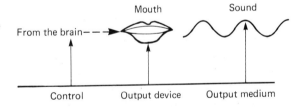

What other output devices do you have, and what medium do they use? This list has already been started for you – see if you can add to it in your workbook.

	OUTPUT DEVICE	MEDIUM
1	Mouth	Sound
2	Hand	Movement

Now let's look at a picture of you to show how the input, the controlling brain, and the output work together:

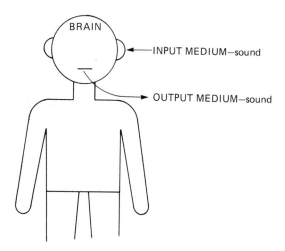

BRAIN

INPUT MEDIUM—sound

OUTPUT MEDIUM—sound

When new information arrives in your brain, you store it in your *MEMORY*; in other words, you remember it. If you're only going to want it for a short while, memory is the best place to keep it. However if you'll be needing it later on and you think that you're in danger of forgetting it, you'll probably decide to store it somewhere else; for example, you might write it down in a notebook. This notebook is a form of *BACKING STORAGE* – somewhere to keep things which you don't trust yourself to remember.

What other methods of backing storage can you think of? This list has already been started for you – see if you can add to it in your workbook.

METHOD OF BACKING STORAGE

1 Notebook
2 Photograph

All these different parts of *you*, acting together – input devices, output devices and memory, with information being stored and processed under the control of your brain, are called a *SYSTEM*. Let's look at a familiar situation and see how the different parts of your system work together to deal with it.

1 Your friend calls you 'a silly fool'.

2 This information is *input* to your ear in the form of sound, and then passed on to your brain, where it is stored in your *memory*.

3 Your brain *processes* this information by thinking it over and deciding that it doesn't like it. It then has to continue processing in order to decide what action to take, if any.

   (Notice that there are two different parts in your brain: the *processor*, which is controlling what is going on and taking decisions, and the *memory*, which is simply storing information.)

Let's look at what has happened so far:

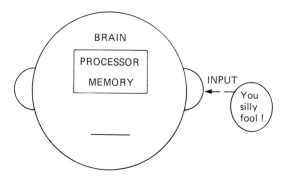

BRAIN

PROCESSOR

MEMORY

INPUT

You silly fool !

4 What happens next will depend on
   a) how annoyed your brain is is by the information it has received, and
   b) the memory of what you have done on similar occasions in the past and how well it has worked.

   If you decide to make a mild reply, your brain will transmit a message to one of your *ouput* devices, in this case, your mouth. You might then say 'That

4

was a rude thing to say.' This message will be output using the medium of sound. We can now add to our picture:

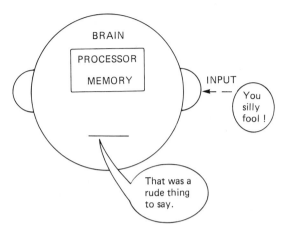

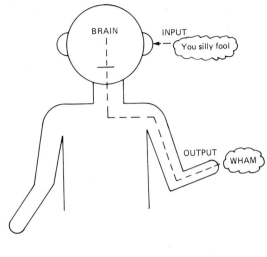

You might want to take stronger action than this. Perhaps you decide to complain to the teacher or lecturer and try to get your friend punished; in that case, it will probably be important to have an exact record of what was said. To do this, you find a piece of paper and write down your friend's comment word for word. What you have now done is to copy the piece of information which was originally input on to backing storage so that you will be able to find it again at any time and repeat it accurately.

If neither of these courses of action appeals to you, you might decide on a more direct approach to the problem. Your brain may have come to the conclusion that your so-called 'friend' deserves a punch on the nose. In this case your brain will transmit a message to a different output device – your hand – which will then deliver the punch.

Things to do

1 Look at the illustration overleaf which shows a simplified human being and some of his or her input and output devices. As you see, they are all connected to the brain. Draw the diagram yourself in your workbook and add as many more devices as you can.

2 For each of the following situations, name the input devices, name the output devices, and draw a diagram in your workbook to show how the information is *transmitted* (passed from one to the other).

a) You are in a cold room. Your hands and feet tell your brain that they are cold. Your brain tells your hands and feet to move in order to keep warm.

b) The same situation as a), but your brain transmits a message to your mouth to tell someone to put the fire on.

c) You see two bars of chocolate in a

5

shop. They are priced at 20p and 35p. You have 60p in your pocket. You do a quick sum in your head, decide that you have enough money, and hand it over to the shop-keeper, asking for both bars.

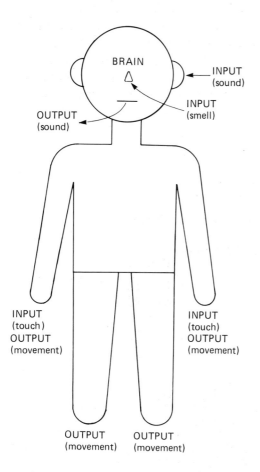

Does a computer work in the same way?
Let's look now at a simple computer and see how the way it works compares with the way you work.

A computer can	INPUT	information
	PROCESS	information
	REMEMBER	information
	STORE	information
and	OUTPUT	information

because it's made up of the parts like ourselves. This diagram shows how these parts work together.

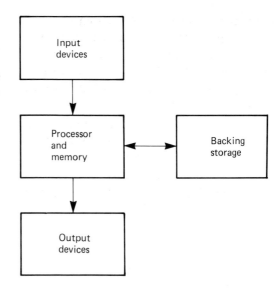

A very simple form of computer could consist of the following devices:

1 *An input device – the keyboard*
In appearance, this is similar to a typewriter keyboard. It is used to input information to the computer. The information is typed into it in the form of letters or numbers, and the keyboard then changes what has been typed into a pattern of electronic pulses. From now until the results of the processing are output, the computer will handle the information electronically. Interestingly, our own brains too operate by a type of electronic pulse.

2 *A processor and memory – the Central Processing Unit (CPU)*
This will be made up of electronic 'circuitry'; that is, electronic components powered by a flow of electricity which work together to act as the 'brain' and 'memory' of the computer. It is known as the Central Processing Unit (CPU) and holds both the processor and the memory functions. It may come in a separate case of its own, or may live in the same case as one of the other devices as in the picture.

3 *An output device – the monitor*
This is similar to a television screen; in fact some very small computers use a television for this. The computer displays information on the screen, in the form of letters, numbers or pictures. This is how it outputs information to you. The screen is also useful when you are inputting information at the keyboard, since it displays back to you everything which you have typed. It may be either attached to a keyboard or self-contained, as in the picture.

4 *A backing storage device – the cassette recorder*
The computer uses this for holding all information which it doesn't have room to keep permanently in its memory. The recorder and the cassettes used are ordinary domestic ones, but the information is stored on the tape in a special form which the computer can understand. Then, when something is needed from the tape, the recorder is set playing and the computer 'reads' the information into its memory.

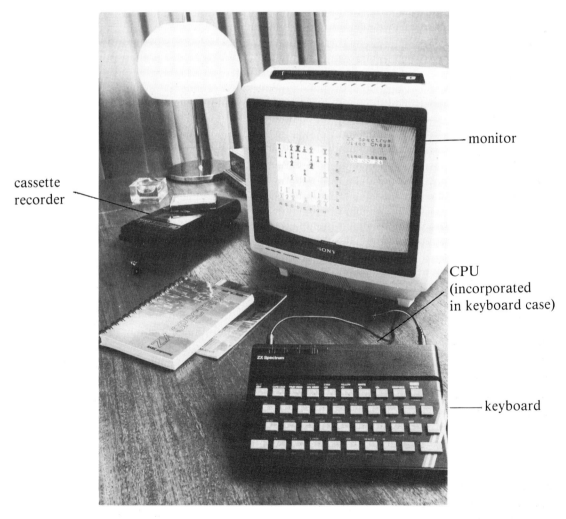

cassette recorder

monitor

CPU (incorporated in keyboard case)

keyboard

The Sinclair ZX Spectrum personal computer

There's a general word which describes these pieces of equipment and others like them. They're all types of *HARDWARE*. Hardware means any kind of computer equipment, from nuts, bolts, wires and electronic parts, to the finished devices.

We've now looked at all the pieces of hardware making up our simple computer system. Let's suppose that they've all been connected together, plugged in and switched on ready for use. Will the system work, do you think? Can we use it to process any information?

The answer is no, not yet. There's still something important missing, and until we've supplied it the computer can't be used. Let's try setting the computer a task and then see if we can work out what else it will need from us before it can perform it.

Suppose we want it to tell you what star sign you are. There will be several steps involved in this:

1   The processor outputs a message on the VDU screen to ask you for your date of birth.

2   You type in your date of birth at the keyboard and it is stored in memory.

3   The processor searches through a cassette on a cassette recorder for a list of the star signs and what dates each one covers. When it finds this information, it reads it into memory.

4   The processor compares your date of birth with the list, and works out what star sign you are.

5   The computer prints this information on the VDU screen:

> What's your date
> of birth?
> 28/10/67
>
> ***You are a Scorpio **

Have you been able to work out what the computer will need from us before it can do this? The answer is, it needs a set of instructions to tell it what to do. Earlier in the chapter we explained that computers can't think of anything by themselves, they can only do exactly what they're told. Until this computer has been instructed how to work out what star sign somebody is, it won't be of any use to you.

A set of instructions telling a computer what to do is called a *PROGRAM*. The instructions have to be written in a special language which the computer can understand. So before the computer could work out your star sign, it would need a program of instructions which would explain how to do it, step by step.

This is where a computer is different from a person. If *you* were asked to work out someone's star sign, you could probably do it without help. If you didn't already know what the different signs were, you could look them up in a magazine or newspaper. You wouldn't need a special program, the necessary instructions would already be in your memory.

Not always, though. Here is a list of different things to do. Which ones do you know how to do already, and which ones would you need extra instructions for?

1 Changing a spark plug

2 Multiplying eight by ten

3 Cooking a chocolate steamed pudding

4 Getting married

5 Using a video recorder

6 Opening a tin

7 Putting up a tent

8 Driving a car

Probably you would need to be told how to do at least one of the things on the list; in other words, you would need a program of instructions to follow. Recipes and instruction manuals are something like computer programs.

Unlike a computer, however, you could have a try at most of these things even without proper instructions. Of course, you might get some odd results. The pudding might be burnt, you might drive the car into a tree, the tent could fall down in the night, and you might end up getting divorced rather than getting married! But whatever happened you would have started to learn how the job should be done. Next time, (if there was a next time), you would probably try a different way of doing it, which might

work better. In the end, if you survived that long, you would probably have worked out a good method simply by trial and error.

Our brains are very good at making decisions, and at solving problems in all sorts of different ways. We might end up with twenty different recipes for chocolate steamed pudding, or more than one way to open a tin. Different people will work out their own methods for whatever you ask them to do. A computer, however, can't do this. It can only follow the program of instructions which it has been given. If the instructions aren't very clear, or have been badly worked out, the computer won't do the job very well, because it's only as good as the instructions were in the first place.

We've already seen that computer equipment is called *HARDWARE*. The programs which are needed to tell the hardware what to do are called *SOFTWARE*. Both HARDWARE and SOFTWARE are needed for a working computer system.

Now let's go back to the exercise on page 5, where you have 60p to buy two bars of chocolate which cost 20p and 35p. How would a computer go about working out whether you can afford them? See if you can list the steps it might take; then compare your list with the one below.

1 You give the processor a program which tells it what it will have to do. The program is read into memory from cassette tape.

2 The processor prints a message on the VDU screen to ask you how much the bars cost.

3 You type in the cost of the two bars, which is then stored in memory.

4 The processor prints a message to ask you how much money you have.

5 You type in the amount, which is then stored in memory.

6 The processor adds together the 20p and 35p and compares it with the 60p.

7 The result, (that you have 5p left), is printed on the VDU screen.

> How much do the bars cost?
> 1st bar is? 20p
> 2nd bar is? 35p
> How much money do you have?
> 60p
> You can buy the chocolate bars, and you will have 5p over.

Things to do

1 Fill in, *in your workbook*, the missing words in the following sentences. *Do not mark the book.*

  a) A computer receives information through its ----- -------.

  b) The information received is then stored in ------.

  c) Information to be kept for a long time is usually put in ------- -------.

  d) The information is dealt with by the ----------.

  e) The brain of the computer, which is made up of the processor and the memory together, is called the -------- --------- ----.

  f) When a computer does a job, it is following a ------- of instructions.

  g) Computer equipment is called --------.

  h) Computer programs are called --------.

2 Earlier, (page 2), you were asked to draw (in your workbook) a simple diagram of a computer. Now that you know more about computers, try and draw a more detailed one.

3 List the steps a computer would need to take to work out how many days there are in the current month.

What does a computer look like?

You have seen by now that a computer isn't just a simple black box; instead, it's a complicated machine which is made up of lots of different parts. Because of this, no two makes of computer will look exactly the same.

One reason for this is the number of different input, output and storage devices which are used by computers. So far, we have only looked at a few simple ones, but there are many others. A general name for them all is *PERIPHERALS*. A peripheral is any device used by the CPU.

You already know of some computer peripherals. Make a list of as many as you can, and whether they are input, output or backing storage devices. Compare your list with other people's lists, and see how many you have thought of between you.

Let's look briefly at some common peripherals. Many of these will be explained in more detail in later chapters.

Input devices

All of these accept information and change it into electronic form before passing it through to the CPU for processing. The photographs show some common input devices and input media.

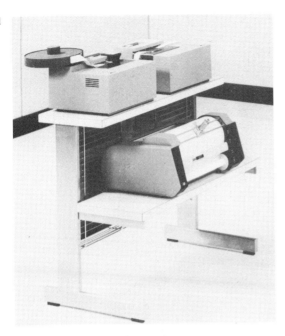

1 A paper-tape reader (with punch)
2 Paper-tape
3 Card reader
4 Punched cards

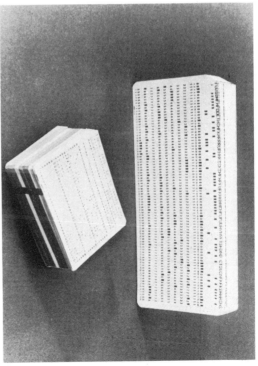

A bar code

A teletypewriter

IBM 3660 Supermarket System
Items are either keyed in by the checkstand attendant or read by a high-speed optical scanner – the IBM 3666 – which can scan and enter information on items carrying a machine readable item code.

As an item is pulled across the scanner's window, a laser beam reads, the system automatically decodes and registers, the information on the symbol. This can bring a higher degree of accuracy and speed to the checkout process.

Storage devices and storage media

1 A floppy disc drive
2 Reel-to-reel tape deck
3 Hard disc and drives and hard discs
4 A hard disc

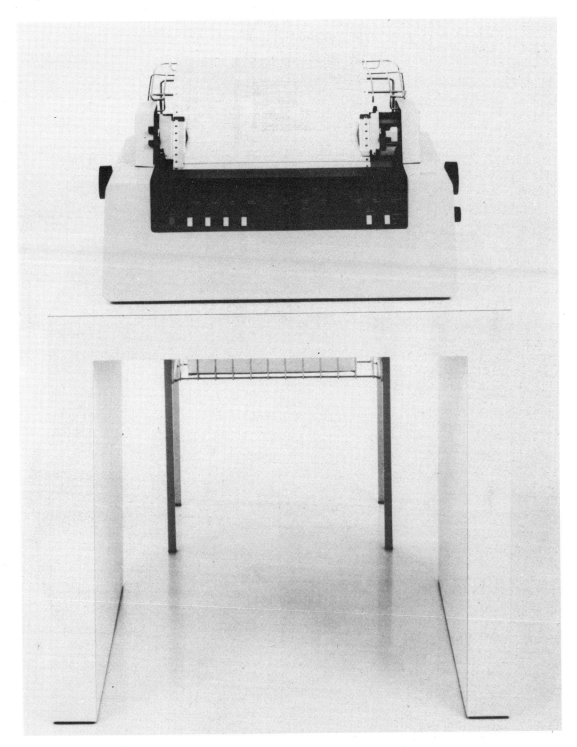

IBM 5256 Printer-matrix

IBM 3800 Printing System

Now let's look at how all these different devices work together with a CPU to form a complete computer. To do this we need to consider more than one size of computer. There are three sizes altogether:

1 Microcomputers
These are the smallest and cheapest computers. There's often no more to

them than the CPU, a keyboard, a VDU and a cassette recorder. You may have seen this type of computer being sold in local shops, or someone you know may have one at home. These computers can be carried around, and are often called 'desk-top' computers. They can be found in use in such places as the home, at school or college, in laboratories or in small businesses; however they're not suitable for use where there's a great deal of processing to be done.

The photograph below shows one of the cheapest microcomputers available at the moment (1984), the Sinclair ZX Spectrum.

2 Main-frame computers
These are the largest and most expensive computers. Main-frames are larger than other sizes of computer, cost more, and can process information at a faster speed. They generally have a great many powerful peripherals, as well as a lot of storage space and a fast and powerful processor. They usually need their own large room to hold all the different pieces of equipment, their own power supply, an air conditioning unit, and a team of specially trained staff to operate them. On the other hand, they are capable of doing a great deal of work at a very fast speed. They are generally found in large organizations which need a lot of processing done, such as big companies and government departments. Different devices can be linked together across long distances by telephone lines, which makes them very useful to organizations which are spread out geographically.

3 Minicomputers
These are the middle range of computers. They generally have more peripheral devices and greater processing power than microcomputers, although their capabilities don't match up to main-frames. Minicomputers are usually found in small businesses, in departments of large organizations, or controlling industrial processes.

ICL ME 29 Model Computer

IBM 4341 – a main-frame computer

18

What can a computer do?

Once a computer has been properly programmed, the list of jobs it can do is almost endless. Here are just a few examples; we'll be looking at some of these in more detail in later chapters.

A computer can:

STORE   information ready for later use – letters, books, information about company profits, details of scientific experiments, pictures, and many other kinds;

PROCESS   information into any form needed – rearrange words or sentences, sort out numbers, do calculations, search for particular pieces of information;

SEND MESSAGES   across short or long distances, either to people or to other computers;

CONTROL   other machines, and processes – for instance, on the shop floor in industry.

Things to do

1 List as many ways as you can in which information can be *input* to a computer. Try and include some ways which aren't given in this chapter.

2 Name *four* things which a computer *wouldn't* be good at, and *four* things which it would. Give reasons for each.

3 Make a list of any local organizations or businesses which you know of. Then write down which size of computer you think would be most suitable for each, and why.

2

Operating a microcomputer

What will this chapter teach you?

This chapter gives you step-by-step instructions on how to operate a microcomputer, which involves the following tasks:

1 **recognizing** the different devices which are necessary in order to set up a microcomputer system, and finding out what each is used for;

2 **linking up** the devices correctly, and switching on and checking the system ready for use;

3 **making** correct use of the computer keyboard;

4 **selecting and loading** a program from a storage medium such as cassette tape or disc;

5 **running** the program, reacting correctly to any instructions it gives or input it requires;

6 **switching off** the computer system at the end of the session.

Introduction – getting ready to start

To follow the instructions given in this chapter, you will need access to a microcomputer. Your school or college should have one available for you to use, or if you are lucky you may have one at home.

This chapter is based around the BBC microcomputer, which has been chosen because it is one of the standard machines used in schools and colleges. If your computer is of a different type, however, you may still find this chapter helpful. Most microcomputers work in a similar way to one another, so the instructions given here will apply in a general way to almost any of them, although small details will be different on different machines. Your teacher will be able to tell you about these differences.

The instructions are provided in the form of a series of steps, which will take you through the various stages of operating a microcomputer and give you exercises to do to make sure that you're getting it right. It doesn't matter if you don't have time to go through all the steps in one session, you can always jump ahead to the last one, which explains how to switch off, and come back another time. If you're following a course, there will probably be a teacher or a technician around to help you out with any problems; if you're not, you will find it useful if you can arrange to have an experienced person in the background when you start.

Steps 1-3 Getting to know your computer

Step 1
Look carefully at the computer which you will be using. It will probably be standing on a desk or table, with various linked pieces of equipment around it.

Now see if you can answer the following questions:

a) Where is the *Central Processing Unit* (CPU)?

b) How is data *input* to the computer?

c) How does the computer *output* information?

d) What medium does it use for *backing storage*?

e) What is each piece of equipment that you can see called?

If you have trouble with any of the questions, you should be able to answer them if you read through chapter 1 again.

Step 2
Look at the illustration which shows a BBC computer. Draw a simple diagram in your workbook showing your own microcomputer, the various devices attached to it, and how they all link up to one another.

The minimum equipment you are likely to be using is as follows:

BBC microcomputer

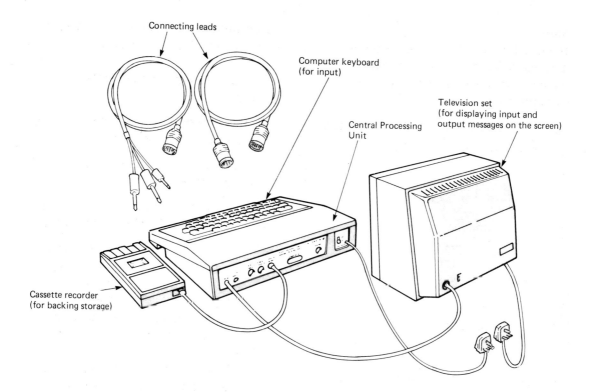

Connecting leads

Computer keyboard
(for input)

Central Processing
Unit

Television set
(for displaying input and
output messages on the screen)

Cassette recorder
(for backing storage)

i)   a microcomputer with a keyboard;

ii)   a display screen (on many
      microcomputers, this is part of the
      main computer, but the BBC
      computer uses a television screen
      attached separately);

iii) a cassette recorder.

You may also have a printer, for
producing written documents, or a disc
drive, which is a backing storage device;
these will be explained in more detail later
on.

Step 3
Before you can go any further, it is
important to check that all connecting
leads are properly in place. If any are not,
find out how to plug them in, from your
teacher or from the instruction manual
which goes with the computer, and then
plug them in correctly.

You are now ready to start up your
microcomputer.

Steps 4 – 5 Starting up

Step 4
Switch on your microcomputer system.

i)   Plug in all the pieces of equipment to a
      mains electricity supply, and ensure
      that all plugs are *ON* (you may find
      that this has already been done for
      you).

ii)   Switch on your microcomputer. The
      BBC microcomputer has a flat
      ON/OFF switch at the back.

iii) Switch on any other devices which are
      linked up to the computer: the
      television, the printer, the cassette
      deck (if it has an *ON/OFF* switch) etc.

Step 5

If everything is working correctly, a message or character will appear on the screen. The screen of the BBC computer will look like this:

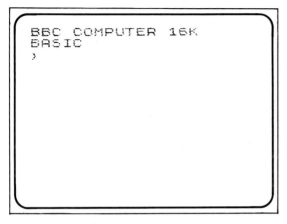

```
BBC COMPUTER 16K
BASIC
>
```

(The details of the screen layout will vary according to the type of BBC computer you are using; there are slight differences between them.)

16K is a message telling you how large a memory the computer has, BASIC is the name of the language which the computer will be using, and > is a symbol which indicates that the computer is waiting for input from you.

You'll also notice a small flashing bar. This is called the *CURSOR*, it tells you where you are on the screen.

If nothing at all appears on the screen, there are several likely reasons:

a) the electricity is switched off at the mains;

b) the microcomputer or the television set has not been switched on;

c) the television is not correctly connected to the computer;

d) the television is not correctly tuned in to receive signals from the computer;

e) (this is the most unlikely reason) one or more pieces of equipment are faulty.

If you can't see what the problem is, check the instruction manual which goes with the computer or ask the teacher or technician.

When the system is working correctly, you are ready to learn how to use the keyboard.

Step 5 – 6 Learning to use the keyboard

Step 5

Look at the keyboard of your computer. The BBC keyboard looks like this.

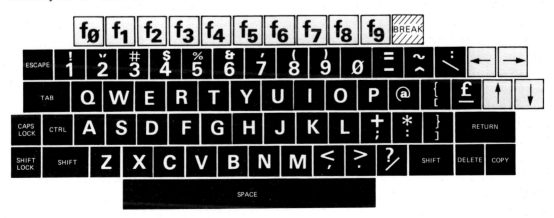

If you're using some other type of computer, you'll notice that your keyboard is slightly different. Keys will be in different positions, or have different names, or may not be there at all. You should still be able to follow most of these instructions, but when you do the exercises you'll need to search to find out which keys correspond to those shown here.

Step 6

We're now going to consider the keys in groups. As they're explained to you, try them out. You can't do any harm by this. Sometimes the computer may put a puzzled message on the screen to tell you that you've made a mistake and that it doesn't understand what you've just typed in!

Group 1 – Alphabetic characters

These are in the same positions as on a standard typewriter keyboard. The bar which you can see below them is called the *space bar* and will give you a space on the screen whenever you press it.

If you want to type in capital letters as well as small ones, there are three ways of doing this:

a) Check that the red light underneath the keyboard labelled CAPS LOCK is on; if not, press the *CAPS LOCK* key, which will make it come on. All the time that this light is on, any letters which you type in will come out as capitals (caps).

b) Check that the red light underneath the keyboard labelled SHIFT LOCK is on; if not, press the *SHIFT LOCK* key to make it come on. All the time that this light is on, any letters which you type in will come out as capitals. This lock also has an effect on other keys, which will be explained when we come to look at those keys.

c) When you are pressing the character which you want to be in capitals, hold down one of the two keys labelled *SHIFT* at the same time. Using *SHIFT* also has an effect on some other keys on the board.

Try out the keys which have been described. Type in your name – or your favourite football club – or anything else which interests you.

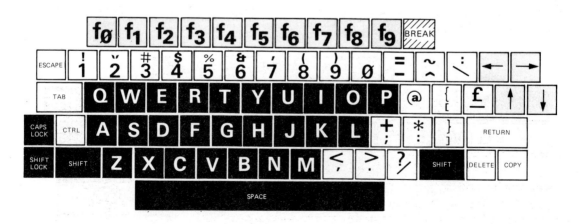

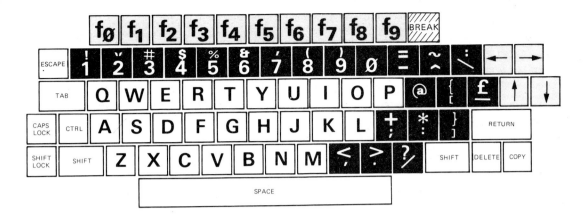

Group 2 – Numbers, punctuation marks, and other non-alphabetic characters

You'll notice that almost all of these keys have *two* symbols shown on them, not one. Which of these appears on the screen when the key is pressed depends on the use of the SHIFT and SHIFT LOCK keys. If SHIFT LOCK is on, or the SHIFT key is held down, the *top* symbol on the key will be the one shown; otherwise it will be the bottom one.

Try out these keys. Mix them up with the ones which you have already learnt, by typing in your address and telephone number. Make sure that you understand the uses of SHIFT, SHIFT LOCK and CAPS LOCK; go back over the instructions if necessary.

Group 3 – Other important keys

i) The *RETURN* key
Whenever you type something in to the computer, you will need to press this key to send the message through to the CPU. If you have typed in a message which appears on the screen but seems to be having no effect, it will usually be because you have forgotten to press RETURN afterwards.

ii) The *DELETE* key
Pressing this moves the cursor backward and 'wipes out' the character which you have just typed in.

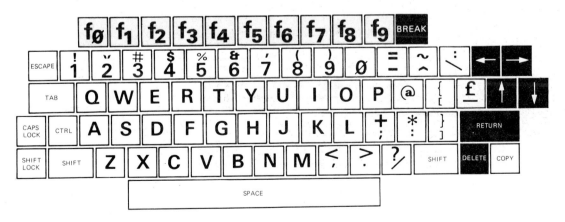

iii) The *CURSOR CONTROL* keys
These are the four arrows on the right-hand side of the keyboard. You won't be using them for the moment; however, when you reach the stage of doing complicated operations such as word processing, you will find these are used to move the cursor around the screen.

iv) The *BREAK* key
This interrupts any program which you are running and wipes it out of memory, clearing the screen at the same time. Be careful about using this one when you are writing or running a program, or you may lose your work.

Type in the following practice lines, take no notice of any messages which appear on the screen:

I AM USING THE MICROCOMPUTER'S KEYBOARD RETURN

DO 1 AND 1 MAKE 2 ? RETURN

I CAN TYPE ALL THESE : *,£,(,   ,/ AND EVEN +. RETURN

When you are confident that you know where all the keys are and how to use them, you will be ready to learn how to load and run a program.

Steps 7 – 11 Loading and running a program

Step 7
Before you can try out one of the uses to which your computer can be put, you will need to give it a program of instructions. These will be in a special language called *BASIC*. The BBC computer has an understanding of BASIC built in; with some other types of computer, BASIC

rules and grammar have to be loaded in before you can go any further. Your teacher will explain what instructions your own computer needs.

Programs are identified by names. You may be told the name of the one which you are going to use, or there may be a choice. You need to ensure that you have been given a copy of the program to be run, on a suitable storage medium for the computer which you are using. The medium will usually be cassette tape but if your computer uses a disc drive as a backing storage unit, then programs will be stored on a small disc, called a floppy disc.

Step 8
Put the cassette into the cassette recorder (or insert the disc into the disc drive) making sure first that it is the right way up. Cassettes must be rewound completely and the tape counter then set back to zero.

Next, find out where on the tape the program which you require is to be found – get the tape counter reading if possible – and wind the tape on until it is positioned just *before* that point.

Step 9
Let's suppose that the program which we will be using is called MEET. This is a simple introductory program for first-time users, which is available on the BBC computer and can easily be adapted to run on other micros. To copy this program from backing storage into memory, type the following instruction:

`LOAD "MEET"`

`RETURN`

LOAD is an instruction which tells the computer to copy a program into memory,

MEET is the name of the program to be copied. The program name must always be put in double quotation marks,

`RETURN`

sends the message through to the CPU, which will then search for the program on the backing storage device.

Step 10
Press the PLAY button on your cassette recorder.

The computer should now load in the program. This may take half-a-minute or so if you are loading from cassette; disc drives are very much faster. The BBC computer prints out messages on the screen while the program is being loaded. You will know when the process is complete, since the computer will print its 'awaiting input' symbol on the screen again.

On the BBC computer, the whole procedure will look something like this:

Step 11
Type the following instruction:

`RUN`   `RETURN`

This tells the computer to begin following the program of instructions which it has loaded into memory; in other words, it is the GO command.

The program which you are running will now take over the job of telling you what to do. Instructions will appear on the screen when they are needed.

If the computer does not respond correctly to RUN, this probably means that the program was not successfully loaded into memory. There are several possible reasons for this; for example, the program might not have been there on the storage medium, or the computer might not be receiving signals from the cassette recorder successfully. Ask your instructor to help find out what is going wrong.

When the program has finished running, the > message will appear on the screen again to tell you that the computer is ready for the next instruction. The program which you have just been using is still in memory, and can be rerun simply by typing in RUN again, or you may want to try loading and running another program.

Short instructions such as RUN and LOAD "MEET" are called *commands*. Here are some more useful ones:

NEW This wipes the current program from memory.

OLD If you have accidently lost the program which was in memory, for example by typing BREAK, typing this immediately will retrieve the program.

LIST This command causes the program in memory to be printed on the screen.

Remember – whether you're typing in a command or following program instructions, RETURN must always follow whatever you've typed.

Step 12 – Switching off the computer

This is the easiest part of all. Simply switch off all the devices which you have been using, and unplug them at the mains if no-one else will be using them. Remove the tape, or the disc, and put it back in its original container. That's all there is to it!

Things to do

1 Explain what each of the following keys is used for:

a) RETURN

b) CAPS LOCK

c) SPACE

d) DELETE

e) BREAK

2 Practise going through the sequence of instructions given in this chapter until you can start up the computer and load and run programs without needing to look at the book.

3

Making the computer work for you

What will this chapter teach you?

This chapter will explain how a simple computer program works. It will not turn you into a programmer but will help you to understand computers better and to use them more confidently. As you work through the chapter, you will be doing the following:

1 **discovering** more about what a computer program is, and exploring the way in which it works;

2 **looking at** ways of describing programs, using diagrams called flowcharts;

3 **learning** some of the rules of a programming language called BASIC;

4 **finding out** about some other programming languages.

---

1 Why should you learn about programming?

Many people are worried at the idea of trying to program a computer. It's often thought that computer programs are difficult and technical, and that only very clever people can understand them.

There is some truth in this. To be able to use a computer language really well, you need training and practice, and it helps if you have the kind of the mind that enjoys trying to work things out logically. However you don't need to be an expert programmer to enjoy programming. Almost anyone can learn to write a simple program in only an hour or two, and many people find that they want to go on from there and learn more.

This chapter won't teach you to be a programmer – the chances are that you'll never need to be one. What it will do is to tell you what computers are and how they work, and then show you how to put together a simple program in a language called BASIC. When you've done that, you'll be able to understand something about the computer programs which you buy and run on your computer; how they're written, and what they do. If you're interested in the subject and want to know more than that, you'll need to get one of the many books on BASIC available from your local library or bookshop.

2 What is a program?

In chapter 1 we saw that a computer program is a set of instructions which is stored in a computer's memory and which tells it what to do, step by step. Let's go back to the comparison we made between ourselves and a computer to help us to understand how a program works.

Do you ever follow a program?

In some ways, yes. There are times when most of us work almost automatically, without giving much thought to what we are doing because it is something we know well. When we do this, we are behaving in a *programmed* way.

One example of an activity which many of us do almost automatically is getting up in the morning. This is probably because we're not awake enough to think about what we're doing and so simply follow the same routine every day. We can think of getting up in the morning as a process which is carried out by our bodies and directed by a set of instructions held in our brain. Input messages are sent to our brain – for example, the sound of the alarm ringing – and the brain responds by producing output in the form of messages to the body telling it to take action.

What instructions are you following when *you* get up? Perhaps they're something like those shown in the picture opposite.

Notice that the *order* in which you follow these instructions is very important. Consider what would happen if:

a) Instruction 8 was done before instruction 7.

b) Instruction 1 was missed out.

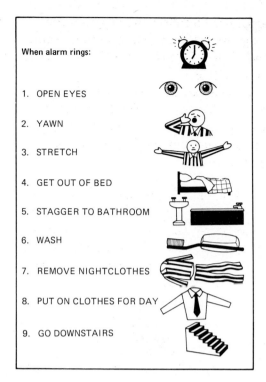

When alarm rings:

1. OPEN EYES
2. YAWN
3. STRETCH
4. GET OUT OF BED
5. STAGGER TO BATHROOM
6. WASH
7. REMOVE NIGHTCLOTHES
8. PUT ON CLOTHES FOR DAY
9. GO DOWNSTAIRS

It's also important that the instructions are *accurate*. Probably the set of instructions given here wouldn't work exactly for you; things are done slightly differently in your house. If you were to try to follow them, you'd run into difficulties; for instance, you might not have an alarm clock. The instructions would not be accurate for *your* getting-up process.

As well as being accurate and in the right order, the instructions need to be sufficently *clear* to follow. For example, instruction 6 would probably need to be spelt out in more detail for a small child who didn't know how he or she was expected to wash; and a guest in a strange house couldn't follow instruction 5 without being told where the bathroom was.

The instructions must also be given in a form which you can understand; in other words, they must be in a *language* which you know. To follow the program for getting up, we need to know the meaning of words like OPEN, YAWN, STRETCH and STAGGER.

We use all kinds of languages in our everyday lives, not foreign languages like French or German, but special ways of giving instructions. Let's look at a few examples of this:

1.   K 4 * K.1.S.1.P.S.S.O * rep from * to *

Do you recognize this? It's a line from a knitting pattern. It tells the person making a garment what stitches to use and in what order to knit them.

2.   'Promenade around the hall,
        Do-si-do your partners all!'

If you were at a country dance, there'd be someone at the front of the hall calling out instructions like this to you, to tell you what steps you should be dancing.

3.   ATTENTION!.
    BY THE LEFT, QUICK, MARCH !
            RIGHT WHEEL !
            SQUAD HALT !
          STAND AT EASE !

These are parade-ground instructions, used in drilling soldiers.

Not all of these special languages are written or verbal. A shepherd whistling to his dog, telling it how to round up the sheep, is using his own language. So is a person at an auction who raises a newspaper to make a bid. The important thing is that everybody concerned – both the person giving the instructions and the person following them – understands the language being used. If you wanted to learn to knit, or to country dance, or to whistle up sheep dogs, you would first have to learn the meaning of the special instructions and how to use or follow them yourself.

Computer programs also have to be written in a special language. There are several different languages available for most computers. In this chapter, we're going to be looking at a language called BASIC.

Can computer programs take decisions?
Yes.

31

To understand how, let's first of all go back to our 'getting-up-in-the-morning' program and see how *you* might go about making a decision. The program could be changed to:

When alarm rings:

1 OPEN EYES

2 YAWN

3 STRETCH

4 *Is it a week day?*

5 If the answer is no,   GO BACK TO SLEEP.

6 If the answer is yes,   GET OUT OF BED
                            STAGGER TO BATH-ROOM
                            WASH
                            REMOVE NIGHT-CLOTHES
                            PUT ON CLOTHES FOR DAY
                            GO DOWNSTAIRS

In line 4 of this program, you are asking yourself a question. If the answer is no, you are taking one action; if the answer is yes, you are taking a different set of actions. Computers can be programmed to behave in exactly the same way as this when they have to decide something. They ask a question, and the answer to that question decides what processing they will do.

Things to do

1 Write a program of instructions for going to bed at night.

2 Make a list of special languages which we use to give each other instructions. Try to include some which aren't given in this chapter. Can you think of any reasons why we should develop special languages instead of always using straightforward English?

3 Imagine that you are about to take a bath. Write down all the different decisions you would have to make from entering the bathroom to getting into the bath.

3 What is a flowchart?

It is often useful to draw a diagram showing how a program of instructions will work. Diagrams of this kind are called *FLOWCHARTS*. They can be used to illustrate any instructions, whether they are for a person or a computer. A flowchart is used to describe the *logic* of a program; that is, how the different instructions fit together. Once you've learned to read flowcharts, you'll probably find them quicker and easier to understand than written programs.

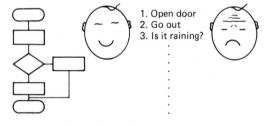

How are flowcharts drawn?
Flowcharts are made up of standard boxes. Let's look at the most important ones and see how they can be used together to show the logic of a program.

1 The START / END box

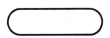

This is the easiest box of all. A START box is put at the beginning of every flowchart, and an END box at the finish, like this,

2 The PROCESS box

This box is used to show an *action*. This can be anything, from going for a walk to adding up two numbers. Let's look at an example from everyday life. Suppose Mr Smith wants to put on his coat every evening and walk his dog. First of all, we'll write a program of instructions for this activity. It will be a very simple program:

1. PUT ON COAT
2. WALK DOG

Now let's draw a flowchart to show this:

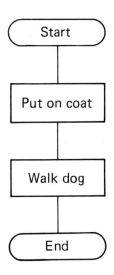

Practise using the start/end box and the process box together by drawing a flowchart for the program of instructions on page 30.

3 The DECISION box

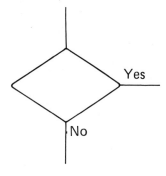

This box is used to show a *decision* being taken between two paths of action. There is one line going into a decision box and two going out. This is because the box always asks a question and gives two possible paths to take, depending on whether the answer to the question is yes or no.

An example will show how this works. We've already drawn a flowchart giving Mr Smith instructions for his evening dog-walking. Now let's suppose that he first looks at the weather and only decides to walk the dog if it is not raining. This

33

means that he will have an extra process to go through – checking the weather – and a question to ask himself – is it raining? – before making the decision.

The program of instructions will now look like this:

---

1 CHECK WEATHER

2 *Is it raining?*

3 If the answer is yes, don't do anything further.

4 If the answer is no,   PUT ON COAT

                      WALK DOG.

Now let's draw a flowchart to illustrate this program:

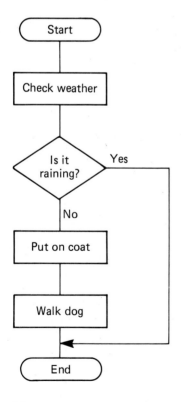

Can you draw a flowchart for the getting-up program on page 32? You'll need to use all three kinds of boxes that you've learned. Try and draw your own, then compare it with the one shown opposite.

'Getting-up' flowchart

Flowcharting that problem was straightforward because only one decision had to be made. Another flowchart is shown opposite, this one of a slightly more complicated situation. Can you work out what would happen if you followed it?

So far, we haven't been looking at *computer* flowcharts, but these are drawn in the same way and using the same kind of boxes as those we've already seen. If a computer program is at all complicated, it is very useful to draw a flowchart of the logic before sitting down to write the program instructions; it helps the programmer to get the way the program will work clear in his or her mind. Flowcharts are so useful that there are many different kinds – we've only looked at one sort. Later on in the chapter we'll be seeing how flowcharting a problem helps when you're writing a computer program.

Things to do

1 A police officer checks the name of a person who is acting suspiciously against a list of wanted persons. If the person is on the list, he or she will be taken to the police station; otherwise, released with a warning.

Draw a flowchart to illustrate this.

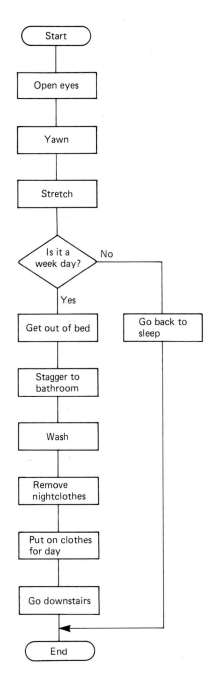

'Getting up' flowchart

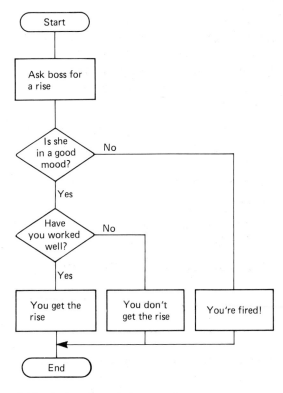

Asking the boss for a rise!

2 Draw a flowchart for one of the following:

   a) the 'buying-a-bar-of-chocolate' problem on page 5;

   b) boiling an egg;

   c) changing a wheel on a car.

4 How does BASIC work?

BASIC is a language for writing computer programs. It uses English words, such as PRINT, IF, THEN, ELSE, and RETURN, but it uses them in a way which has a special meaning to a computer. If you want to give a computer instructions, you have to use a language like this. There isn't, at the moment, any way in which you can give your computer a message in everyday speech, such as 'Please sort these names into alphabetical order for me' and expect to be understood – although one day in the future you might be able to do this.

There are many different computer languages. BASIC (the letters stand for Beginners' All-purpose Symbolic Instruction Code) is designed for people who are new to programming, and is one of the easier ones. Using it, you can give a computer instructions for doing everything from straightforward sorting out of words and numbers to controlling machines in factories.

How do you write a program in BASIC?
Before you can write your first BASIC program, there are a few things that you need to know.

The first one is that programs are written in *lines*, and every one of these must start with a *line number*. This is to tell the computer in what order to follow the instructions. You could number your lines 1,2,3, and so on, but it's better to go up in tens. The advantage of numbering your lines 10, 20, 30, 40 and upwards is that if you've forgotten a line it's easy to put it in afterwards in the right place, using a spare number such as 16.

The second important point is that computers are very fussy about punctuation. You won't be able to get away with missing out things like commas, full stops or quotation marks if the line needs them; the computer won't understand the instruction. Because of this, you'll need to be very careful and accurate when you're typing in a program at the keyboard.

The other thing you need to know is that your computer program will have to be given special places to hold information. These places are called *variables* because the information kept in them varies. You can think of them as drawers in memory which are used to store letters and numbers. There are two types. Those with names ending in a $ sign are for storing *alphabetic* characters only; the others are for storing numbers. (See opposite.) These variables are laid out in an ordered way in computer storage, but it won't matter to you where they are in memory.

BASIC programs can do many different kinds of processing. Two of the most common types are handling text and doing calculations. Let's see how we could write a program to do each of these.
1 Handling text
Suppose that we need a simple program which asks you on the VDU screen for your name, waits until you type it in at the keyboard, and then prints out a message of welcome.

The program might look like the example opposite.

```
10 INPUT A$
20 PRINT "HELLO ";A$;" I AM PLEASED TO MEET YOU"
30 END
```

The *first* line tells the computer that it needs to take in some information from you by way of the keyboard and to store the information you give it in the variable called A$.

The *second* line tells the computer to print on the screen the message of welcome and the information stored in A$.

The *third* line simply tells the computer that the program is finished.

Let's see if it works. Try typing the program into your microcomputer. You will need to type it in line by line, pressing the RETURN key at the end of each line. Remember, it's important to be completely accurate in what you type.

Don't be surprised that nothing happens when you've finished typing. The computer has only stored the instructions in memory; it isn't trying to follow them yet. You've already learned that RUN is the command needed to start a program going, so type RUN now (followed by RETURN).

One of two things will now happen. There may be an error in your typing; in that case, the computer will give you a message to tell you that there's something wrong with one of the lines in the program. If that happens, retype the complete line correctly, and the old line will be automatically replaced. If, however, your typing was accurate, your program will now start running and will output a question mark. This means that it is waiting for you to type in your name. When you have done this (don't forget RETURN !) the computer will print the message of welcome on the screen. The screen might then look like this:

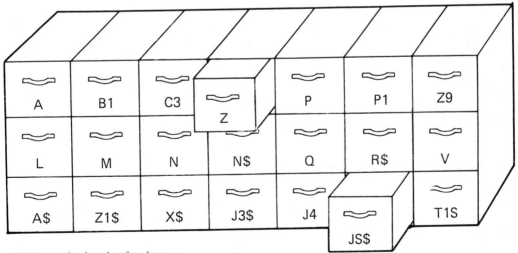

Variables can be thought of as drawers

```
>10  INPUT A$
>20  PRINT "HELLO ";A$;" I AM
     PLEASED TO MEET YOU"
>30  END
>RUN
?ADAM ANT
HELLO ADAM ANT
```

Look at the three lines of the program again, and see if you can work out the rules by which it is written. You should notice the following things:

1 A$ is the name of the variable (drawer) which holds the name which you input when the program is run;

2 the messages which the computer prints around the name held in A$ are surrounded by double quotation marks;

3 the different parts of the message to be printed on the screen are separated by semi-colons.

2 Doing calculations

Suppose we wish to use the computer to convert a distance in kilometres to miles. To do this, we need to work out 5/8th of the distance, which means multiplying it by 0.625.

A BASIC program to do this is shown below:

The *first* line asks you to type in the distance in kilometres at the keyboard, and stores the number you put in in K.

The *second* line multiplies the number in K (that is, the distance) by 0.625 and puts the result in M. (* stands for multiply – we can't use X because it could be confused with the letter X).

The *third* line prints the distance in miles, which is held in M.

Now try this out on your computer.

When you run this program you will find that it is not very 'user-friendly' – that is, it doesn't tell the user what to do very clearly when he or she is sat at the keyboard, or explain what the output is.

If you add some extra lines to the program you can make it much clearer and easier to use. Here is a 'friendlier' version of the program:

```
10  INPUT K
20  LET M=K* 0.625
30  PRINT "DISTANCE IN MILES ";M
40  END
```

```
 5  PRINT "THIS PROGRAM CONVERTS A DISTANCE IN
    KILOMETRES INTO A DISTANCE IN MILES"
 8  PRINT "TYPE IN THE DISTANCE IN KILOMETRES"
10  INPUT K
20  LET M=K * 0.625
30  PRINT "DISTANCE IN MILES IS ";M
40  END
```

Type in the extra lines to the program at the bottom of the screen: they will automatically be inserted into the right places. Now run the program again and see what a difference these statements make.

How do programs make decisions?
So far, we've looked at very simple programs which only contain processes, not decisions. We haven't drawn flowcharts to help us write them because their logic is too simple for it to be worth the trouble. Now, however, we're going to look at a BASIC program which asks questions and takes different actions depending on the answers to those questions. We'll see what instructions a program like this will use, and draw a flowchart to illustrate the logic.

Suppose that we want to write a program which will ask the user's age and then tell him or her whether he or she is legally of age to go into a pub and to have an alcoholic drink. Let's start by drawing a flowchart for this, like the one overleaf.

Now that we can see how the logic should work, we can write the program as on page 40.

You'll see that the decisions in this program are dealt with by an instruction that says *IF* something is true *THEN* do something, and after that *GOTO* another line. If it's not true – for instance, on line 60, if the value of A is *not* either eighteen or larger – then the program won't send control to another line; it will just continue processing with the next line after the one you're on.

Look carefully at the instructions in this program and see how they link up with the logic in the flowchart. *REM* is a new instruction, which stands for REMARK. Any line which starts with REM is not performed by the computer. It is simply a comment on the program put in to tell you what it does.

Now try out the program on your computer.

What other programming languages are there?
A good many ! Let's compare three of the commonest languages and see (on page 41) what they can do:

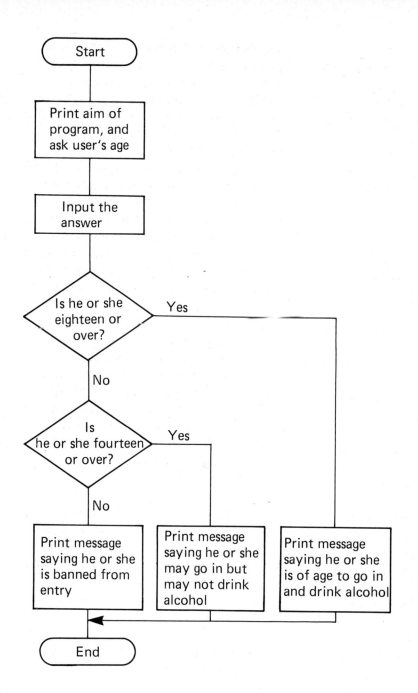

```
10  REM ***** PROGRAM TO DECIDE WHETHER SOMEONE IS OLD ENOUGH *****
20  REM ***** TO GO INTO A PUB AND DRINK ALCOHOL. *****
30  PRINT "THIS PROGRAM WILL TELL YOU WHETHER YOU ARE OLD
ENOUGH TO GO INTO A PUB AND HAVE AN ALCOHOL DRINK"
40  PRINT "HOW OLD ARE YOU"
50  INPUT A
60  IF A>=18 THEN PRINT "YOU MAY GO INTO A PUB AND DRINK ALCOHOL"
:GOTO 90
70  IF A>=14 THEN PRINT "YOU MAY GO INTO A PUB BUT MAY NOT DRINK
ALCOHOL":GOTO 90
80  PRINT "IT IS ILLEGAL FOR YOU TO GO INTO A PUB"
90  END
```

a) *BASIC*

This is the one you've just been using. It's available on almost all microcomputers and most other kinds of computer. It's a general-purpose language, and particularly useful for teaching beginners about programming, although those who become expert generally move on to a language which is able to do more.

b) *COBOL*

This is available on almost all computers except the very smallest ones. It was intended that business managers would be able to understand COBOL programs, so the language is quite near to ordinary English. COBOL is used mainly to write programs which will be used in business.

c) *FORTRAN*

Available on most minis and main-frames – and some micros – this language is designed and used mainly for scientific programming.

These three languages have all been around for a good many years. There are many more recently developed languages, with special uses: LISP, FORTH, PASCAL. . . . the list is long, and growing all the time. There are also other techniques which can replace flowcharts as ways of showing the logic of a program. Nothing stands still for long in the computer world !

One area of programming in which developments have been taking place is *COMPUTER GRAPHICS*; that is, programs to handle pictures. If you've been using a BBC micro, there are many instructions available in BASIC which will draw pictures on the VDU screen; you'll find examples of some on page 78. There are also special languages based around pictures rather than processing numbers and text. One such language is called LOGO. A toy tank called BIG TRAK (see page 42) can be bought which is controlled from a touch-sensitive keyboard, using the principles of LOGO.

Probably most of the programs you will LOAD and RUN on your computer will have been written by somebody else. However, although they are likely to be more complicated than the ones we have been looking at, they will contain the same kind of instructions and work in exactly the same way. What this means is that when a computer is doing a task it's only as good as the person who originally programmed it for that job. Unfortunately, there are some bad programs around. Although you may not be employed as a programmer, you may well be using software written by other people. This means that you have an interest in the quality of the software that you have to work with.

A good program is:

WELL-TESTED – in other words, it should work! Not just some of the time, but as near to all of the time as possible. Any program over a few lines long should have been tried out with a whole variety of different input data before it is handed over to the person who is to use it.

USER-FRIENDLY – it should be clear, easy and helpful to use.

FOOL-PROOF – it should be able to take any data you can throw at it without breaking down or doing something unplanned. It's very easy for someone working at a keyboard to make a mistake in their input. A good program should spot as many of these mistakes as possible.

Big Trak

WELL-DOCUMENTED – there should be instructions or a manual written for it to tell you anything you need to know about how to work it or what it does.

EFFICIENT – this is the most difficult point for the user of a program to judge, but what it means is that the program should be well-structured and no longer than is necessary to do its job.

Things to do

1 Answer the following questions:

a) What must every program line start with?

b) What are variables used for?

c) What is the difference between variables ending with $ and other variables?

d) Name *two* types of processing that BASIC programs can do.

2 *WIN-A-CAR COMPETITION*
A national competition has been run which gives entrants the chance to win a new car. The entry form lists the following features of the car:

A   Reclining seats
B   Low petrol consumption
C   6-year anti-rust guarantee
D   Bolt-on panels
E   Sun roof
F   Stereo cassette player

The person entering has to place these features in order of importance.

It is decided by the competition organisers that the winning combination will be BCDEAF. The entries are to be checked on a computer by a BASIC program. This program will do the following things:

a) read in the name of each entrant;

b) read in his/her entry;

c) check the entry against the correct result;

d) if the entry is a winner, print out the name of the entrant and then WINNER;

e) if the entry is a loser, print out the name of the entrant and then LOSER.

Draw a flowchart to show the logic of this program. Then write the program, type it into the computer, and run it several times until you are sure that it works no matter what input you give it.

4

Meeting the microchip

What will this chapter teach you?
This chapter will introduce you to the microchip and explain why it is important. You'll be working through the following stages:

1 **looking at** how computers worked in the past, and seeing how their technology led to the invention of the microchip;

2 **finding out** what a microchip looks like, what it is made up of, and how it is manufactured;

3 **learning** about the different types of microchip and what they can do;

4 **considering** some of the common uses to which microchips are put in everyday life.

1 What is a microchip?

Now that you've seen how a computer works and had a go at using one yourself, it's time to find out a little more about the technology which makes it all possible. First, have a good look at the computer you have been using. By now you should know what the Central Processing Unit is, and roughly where it can be found. What do you think you would see if you were to unscrew the case and look at the inside of a CPU? A mass of wires? Glass tubes? Rows of black boxes? Flashing lights? Or none of these?

Although the CPU is the brain of the computer, it's often the least impressive part to look at. On microcomputers, as you've seen, it's usually housed in some kind of plain box or case, with perhaps a switch or two and a few lights to be seen on the outside. On more powerful computers – minis and mainframes – the CPU is generally larger, with more controls to be seen, but the outside still doesn't give any clear idea of what it does or how it does it.

A microchip

If you were able to take your CPU to pieces, you would be looking at the *electronic circuitry*; that means a collection of small but powerful electronic components which are linked to each other and work together. These form the brain of the computer.

To understand in detail how they all work, you'd need to read a book on electronics or to take a course in it, but luckily it isn't necessary for you to do that. You can use a computer perfectly well without knowing exactly how the hardware operates, in the same way as you can drive a car without knowing much about what's going on under the bonnet.

There is one type of electronic device, however, that it is useful to know something about. Microcomputers contain quite a few oblong black boxes. These hold very powerful devices indeed, which do most of the work of the computer. Do you know what they are called?

The answer is *MICROCHIPS*. This is another name for 'silicon chips', which you may have heard of or read about. There are many different kinds of them, as we will be seeing later in the chapter. Microchips are so important, both to computers and to other types of machinery, that it's worth spending a chapter finding out exactly what they are and what they can do.

The background

Microchips weren't a sudden invention; the idea didn't just pop up into someone's brain one day. They were the end product of many years work in fields such as electronics and computer science. To understand how the microchip came about, we need first to look at what had happened before it; this means exploring the history of the modern electronic computer.

The idea of the computer isn't new. As early as the nineteenth century someone had the idea of making an automatic machine which had input and output devices, storage, a processing unit, and program control. The name of this inventor was Charles Babbage. In many ways, he was the father of the modern computer, although he was never successful in making the machine which he designed.

Babbage had the right ideas, but he had them at the wrong time – nineteenth-century technology was a long way short of the level that would be needed to build a computer, even of the simple sort that Babbage planned. In those days, there were no such things as electronic components; that was all still in the future. Babbage had to try to build his machine out of *mechanical parts* similar to those shown below.

Parts such as these, if they're made accurately enough (which they weren't in Babbage's day) are used for many types of machinery. Car engines, for instance, are still made from this kind of device. However the processing unit of a computer isn't directly concerned with trying to move heavy parts; it's trying, in a very simple way, to imitate the human

Babbage's machine

brain. To do this with any chance of success, it needs to be complicated, with a great many components. Mechanical parts such as those shown opposite are too heavy and slow-working to be used in the quantities required – a powerful computer which was entirely mechanical, if it could ever be built, would have to be enormous, and it would probably take years to process data!

If technology and science had stayed at the level they were in Babbage's day, we wouldn't have computers now. However the twentieth century brought many important developments, including the widespread use of electricity, and with these changes came the birth of the new science of electronics. This meant a new way of doing things using components which were smaller, cheaper and lighter than mechanical parts. By the 1930's it was beginning to look possible to build a computing machine using this new electronic technology, and this was achieved during the next decade.

In 1939 the Second World War began. In wartime, there were a great many needs for fast processing, to do things like decoding enemy signals or calculating trajectories for shells to produce artillery charts. During this time research into computers gathered speed, and by the end of the war the first fully electronic computers had been built.

The picture overleaf shows ENIAC, one of these early computers. They were built using electronic devices called *valves*. These looked something like small light tubes (you may have seen them in old radios or television sets). The early computers used a tremendous number of them. (See overleaf.)

How do computers like ENIAC compare with those we use today? Let's draw up a table to show where the main

differences are. Before you go through the table, look at the picture again and see how many ways you can think of that ENIAC might have been different from the type of computer you have been using.

Comparing ENIAC with a modern computer
Differences:

1 *Reliability*
   No computer is completely reliable; like all machines, they sometimes break down or go wrong, generally at the most inconvenient moments! The early valve computers were particularly liable to breakdowns. This was mainly due to the valves. These got very hot when they were working, and often failed completely, rather like a light bulb. Computers such as ENIAC contained so many valves that replacing those that failed was a constant problem.

2 *Speed*
   Although using electronic valves was a faster way of processing data than Babbage's idea of mechanical parts, the early computers still did their processing very much more slowly than the ones we use today.

3 *Size and power*
   Early valve computers were very large by modern standards, taking up whole rooms for not much processing power. A present-day computer taking up that much space would be a very powerful main-frame indeed, able to do large jobs of processing at an extremely fast speed. Computers such as ENIAC, however, didn't have much more power than a pocket calculator has now.

ZA 447 Radio valves 1931–1937

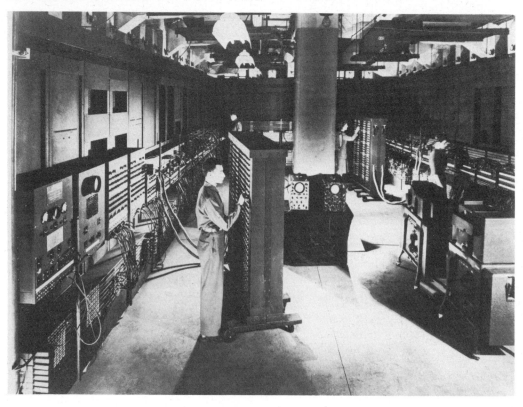

ENIAC – Electronic Numerical Integrator and Calculator

4 Uses

The early computers had much less in the way of input and output devices than present-day ones. Most of the space they took up was because of the large size of their CPU's. They were used mainly for jobs involving a lot of calculations, such as working out figures for military use or analysing codes. Modern computers, on the other hand, being faster, more powerful and with a great many more types of peripheral, can be used for a variety of different purposes, ranging from working out the weather forecast to playing chess; and the number of jobs they can tackle is increasing all the time.

Clearly, valves weren't the perfect device to use in computers. In fact not many people took computers seriously at this time. They were seen as large calculating machines, always breaking down and not of much use outside of university laboratories and military installations. Nobody was to know how changes in technology were to cause the spread of computers in the years to come.

The next important step was the invention of an electronic device called the *transistor*. Unlike valves, transistors are still being used and are as important as ever. They are found in microprocessors, for instance. Several transistors are pictured opposite.

Transistors quickly replaced valves as the main components of computer processors. They could do everything which valves could do, *and* had several advantages over them. Try to make a list of what you think those advantages might be. If you've ever seen or used one of the old-fashioned types of valve radio, and can compare this with a modern transistor radio, you might find that this gives you some clues.

Advantages of transistors over valves
1 *Smaller* – not much smaller, when they were first developed, but over the years their size has continued to diminish,
2 *Cooler* – valves produced a tremendous amount of heat while they were working, which was one of the reasons that they failed so often,
3 *More reliable* – transistors are much more robust than valves, and can take harder treatment,
4 *Cheaper to use* – they don't need as much electricity to drive them as valves do.

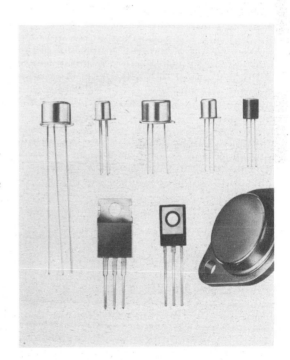

Typical transistor encapsulations

Ferranti radio 1939–44 – a valve set

Philips transistor radio

Micro-miniaturization and the microchip

In the years since the transistor was first invented, electronic circuitry has continued to develop. There have been no really revolutionary changes in the devices themselves; instead, what has happened is that they have got smaller – and smaller – and smaller! First they were miniaturized, then they were *micro-miniaturized*; that is, made microscopically small. We're now at the stage where the entire processing unit of ENIAC could be put on to one tiny chip of silicon and leave room to spare.

That brings us back to your own computer and the silicon chips inside it. What advantages does all this micro-miniaturization bring? Well, it means that your computer has the following characteristics:

1 It's *small*.

Very powerful computers (if we compare them with the computers of just a few years ago) can now sit on top of an ordinary desk, or fit in a brief-case, or live easily inside another piece of equipment.

2 It's *reliable*.

You might argue with this! But although many things can still go wrong with computers, the computer that you've been using can probably be trusted to work correctly for long periods at a time; and when you do have a problem, there's a strong chance that it's due either to a mistake you have made or to something wrong in the software which is built-in to the computer, not to any fault in the hardware.

3 It's *fast*.

In the years since the first electronic computer was made, processing speeds have continued to increase. The circuitry in a microchip is so small that the electricity which powers it has only a very short distance to travel, and it can do this extremely fast.

4 It's *cheap*.

Cheap to *buy* because the microchips in computers are now turned out in large numbers and cost very little. Cheap to *run*, because not much power is required.

This still doesn't mean that you can get a computer for the cost of a pad of paper, but the smallest ones are now cheaper than televisions. What's more, prices are still going down, and nobody knows just how small and cheap computers will be in the future.

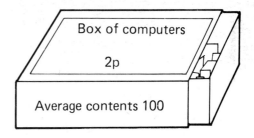

What are microchips made of?

Microchips contain *microelectronic circuitry*; that is, linked electronic components which are very, very tiny. Large numbers of these can be packed tightly on to a single tiny piece of silicon. Silicon is a material found in sand; luckily, it is easy and cheap to obtain. The microchip is made by building up a series of very thin layers of silicon and of the tiny components which are held in it. *Everything* is microscopically small – the transistors, the wiring, and all the other parts which together make up the circuitry.

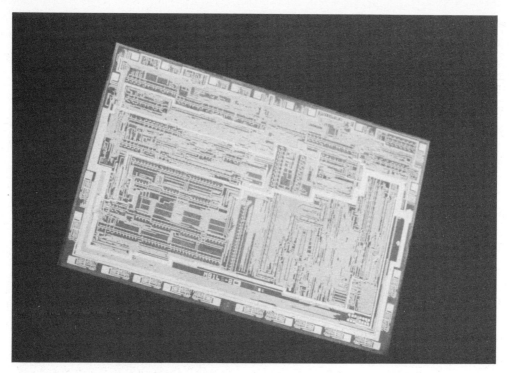

Teletext Acquisition and Control chip

What different kinds are there?

There are three main kinds of microchip:

1 *Microprocessors*

These are the most powerful kind. They are almost tiny computers in themselves. Each one has a processing unit, a memory, and a special area to handle input and output. Microprocessors are the most important part of the CPU of a modern computer. They also have other uses. They are now small enough and cheap enough to be built into many different devices: you can find them in everything from washing machines to toy tanks, providing a simple 'brain' for the machine that uses them.

2 *Memory chips*

These are the commonest form of computer memory. They are used to hold information, either temporarily or permanently.

3 *Input and output chips*

These control the flow of information in both directions.

Things to do

1 Draw an illustrated wall chart to show how computers have changed from Babbage's time up to the present day (you may wish to make this more detailed by looking up further information in an encyclopedia or in a book about the history of computers).

2 Write down *in your workbooks* TRUE or FALSE for each of these statements.

a) Before using a computer, it is important to know exactly how the CPU works.

52

b) Microchips and microprocessors are two words for the same thing.

c) Charles Babbage invented transistors.

d) Mechanical computers are large and slow.

e) When valves are used they get very hot and often fail.

f) The early computers which used valves were mainly bought by shops and factories.

g) Transistors are no longer to be found in computers.

h) Micro-miniaturization has led to cheaper computers.

3 Draw a table comparing mechanical parts, valves, transistors and microchips.

2 How are microchips made?

Because the circuitry in microchips is so small, special methods have to be used to make them. Let's look at how a typical microchip would be manufactured.

Stage 1 – cutting a slice of silicon
A circular slice of silicon, 10 cm by 0.5 mm, is first cut and then polished on one side. This will be used as the base for a number of microchips.

Chips being cut from a disc of oxydised silicon

Stage 2 – coating the slice
The slice of silicon is coated with a special kind of plastic, which is sensitive to light.

Stage 3 – masking
A special 'mask' is put into position over the slice of silicon. There are many of these masks. Each one will have marked out on it the pattern for one layer of the microchip. Because the markings are microscopically small, they will be repeated over and over so that a great many microchips can be built up on one slice of silicon at the same time.

Stage 4 – building up the chips
The covered slice is now treated through the mask to etch away some of the plastic and leave raised patterns. Layers of different materials can then be built up where the plastic was etched away. Finally the rest of the plastic is dissolved away.

Stage 5 – repeating the process
These processes – coating with plastic, masking, etching, building up layers of materials, dissolving the plastic – are repeated over and over again as the circuits are formed. Finally, the electronic components which are needed are added.

Slice pre-test during manufacture of a chip

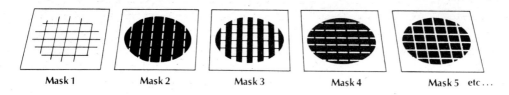

Mask 1   Mask 2   Mask 3   Mask 4   Mask 5   etc...

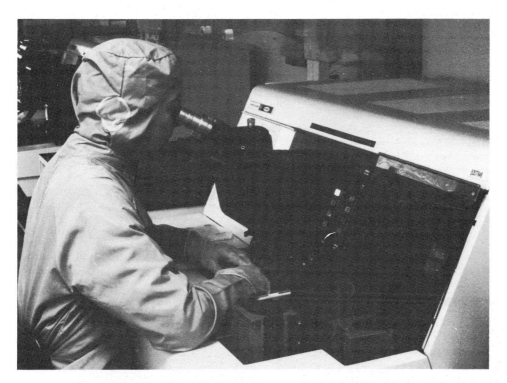

Mask alignment during the manufacture of a chip

Two chips

Stage 6 – checking for errors
The chips on the slice are now machine-tested to check that the circuitry in each works correctly; those that fail this test (most of them) are marked with a spot of paint.

Stage 7 – packaging
The slice of silicon is broken up into individual chips. Those which passed the tests are enclosed in plastic covers, with metal pins which will allow them to be connected with other devices. After a final test, the microchips are ready for use!

How much do microchips cost?

This depends on what type you want to buy. The most expensive thing about making a microchip is the job of designing and testing any new kind. This has to be done before that type of chip can be made in quantity. Once the design has been proved to work, the new chips can be produced in large numbers, and when the cost of designing them has been paid for they can get very cheap. Because of this, a lot of the chips used today are what are called 'industry standards'; that is, they can be used to do all kinds of different jobs. Standard chips are produced in such large numbers that they can cost as little as a few pence each.

On the other hand, if you need a special chip designed to do a particular job for you, it will cost you much more than the standard. The price you pay has to be high because the manufacturer needs to make enough money from you to cover design costs, he or she can't get any of it back by selling that type of chip to other people. Chips which have been designed for a particular job are called 'custom specials'.

Things to do

1 Fill in the missing words *in your workbook* in the following sentences. *Do not mark the book*.

a) Microchips are built up on a slice of -------.

b) The patterned stencils used in building up microchips are called -----.

c) Chips designed for a particular job are called ------ --------.

d) General-purpose chips which can do many jobs are called -------- ---------.

2 Imagine that you work at a microchip factory which produces microchips using the method described in this chapter. Answer the following questions about your work:

a) What needs to be done to slices of silicon before you start building up layers of circuitry on them?

b) How many times during the process of manufacture do you test each chip to be sure that it works?

c) Why do the plastic cases that you put the finished chips into have metal legs?

d) When you find chips that don't work, how do you mark them?

e) Why does your company charge less for the standard chips it makes than it does for specials?

What are microchips used for?

A watch, a toy tank, a cassette recorder, a rocket: they don't seem to have much in common, do they? But the link is that every one contains at least one microchip.

Microchips are not just found in computers. Standard, general-purpose chips are now so cheap that they're being built into a great many different devices. One place that they're becoming common is the home. There's hardly a house now that hasn't got at least one microchip somewhere about. If you go out to buy a new household gadget, there's quite a good chance that you will end up with one that contains a chip.

Think about the kitchen in your home. Microchips may not have affected it yet, but they will. Within a few years, many of us will have kitchens with microprocessor-controlled washing-machines, cookers, fridges, toasters . . . . . the list is long, and it's still increasing.

But what advantages does this give us? Well, building microchips into household appliances gives those appliances memory, processing power and program control. For instance, suppose you want to roast a joint of meat. You might follow a timetable something like this:

1. Switch on oven
2. Set temperature to 375 Fahrenheit
3. Leave for 2 hours
4. Set temperature to 300 Fahrenheit
5. Leave for 1 hour
6. Turn off oven.

As you can see, this is a form of *program*. All these stages would have to be done by hand on the old-fashioned type of cooker, but with the aid of microelectronics this kind of program can be quickly and easily stored and then set running.

But the home isn't the only, or even the most important place, where microchips can be found. Indeed, these days it's not so much a question of listing where they *are* as of trying to think of places where they *aren't*. Small though microchips are - in fact, mainly *because* of their small size and cheapness - they're having a major effect on our society. Microchips are becoming increasingly important in industry, where they're particularly good at controlling other machines and industrial processes of all kinds. They're moving rapidly into offices, where they're changing the nature of the jobs done by secretaries, typists, clerks, and managers. In the home, they've made it possible for people to buy their own personal computers. Everywhere you look, in shops, garages, schools, hospitals, factories and farms, you'll find the microchip as a part of the work being done there. You'll be finding out more about some of these areas, and how microchips fit into them, later in the book.

Things to do

1 Draw up a list of places in which you would expect to find microchips being used, and explain what they would be used for.

2 Suppose that you're selling microchips, trying to persuade the manufacturers of household goods that they should build your chips into them. What do you think are the best selling points of your product?

Husky Hunter – the world's toughest, smallest, large-memory portable computer – in use on a building site

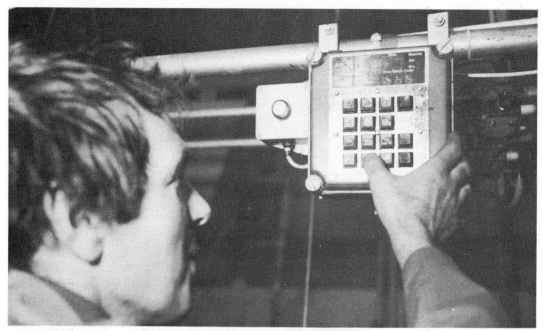

Computer control for feed and book-keeping

Little Green School, Croxley Green, Rickmansworth – operating a programmable robot

Chubb key card

5

Helping in the office

What will this chapter teach you?

In this chapter we begin a look at computers in working life – in businesses, offices and factories – which we will be continuing in chapters 6, 7 and 8. Chapter 5 is about office work and how the computer can help with it. As you work through, you'll be doing the following:

1 **looking at** offices, what happens in them, and the types of staff who work there;

2 **learning** about some of the office machines which staff use to help them do their jobs;

3 **building on** what you've learnt earlier in this book to see why computers can be useful in offices;

4 **finding out** what kinds of computer systems can be commonly found in offices and how they help with the work which is done there.

1 Running an office

Does anyone you know work in an office? Whether it's a relative, a friend or a neighbour, there's probably someone who does. Or have you ever worked in one yourself, during a holiday, perhaps, or as part of a government training scheme? Office work is important, and a great many people do it.

Offices come in all shapes and sizes. They can range from multi-storey blocks to a corner of a room containing just a desk, a telephone and a filing cabinet. The next time that you're in the centre of a town, look around and see how many buildings you can spot that you think contain an office. Some are easy to pick out, like the one shown overleaf. Others are much more difficult; for example, factories and shops usually have a special office section, but it can't always be seen from the outside. By the time you've picked out all the possible buildings, you'll probably be surprised at how many offices there are around, and you may be able to get an idea of just how many people are needed to run them.

An office block

What are offices for?

Although from the outside offices may seem to be simply places where a great many people sit pushing pieces of paper about, there's much more to them than that. Offices are where organizations are run from. Inside any office, all kinds of activities are going on which are aimed at keeping the business of the organization running smoothly and efficiently. Many of the organizations concerned will be commercial businesses, which are carrying on a trade in order to make profits, but there are also other types; for instance government departments, clubs and charities are all concerned with getting a job done, but they may not be trading or trying to make a profit. All of these, however, are likely to need an office to run operations and handle the paperwork which goes along with that.

Until Victorian times, almost all office workers were men. This then began to change slowly. The two world wars speeded things up, since when men joined the armed services women had to do many of the jobs which were left empty. Since that time, women workers have become very important in offices and now outnumber men.

Several different kinds of staff are found in offices. Let's look at each in turn:

1 *Management staff*
These are the people who make the decisions for running the organization. They take the final responsibility for everything which happens within it and for everyone who works there.

2 *Administrative staff*
These are the people who are in charge of the day-to-day running of the organization. Their job is to supervise the general office staff to see that the decisions of the managers are carried out.

60

3 *Clerical staff*

Most people working in offices are clerical staff. They deal with the day-to-day work within the office; answering the telephone, handling the paperwork, filing letters, typing reports, and so on. Let's look at some of the most common clerical jobs and see what kind of work they involve:

Book-keepers keep written records of everything that happens to an organization's money, in special books called *ledgers*.

Shorthand typists take dictation in shorthand and type it up into letters, reports, or whatever else is needed. They may also help with other jobs such as filing.

Clerks are concerned with handling an organization's records – that is, with the paperwork of whatever business the organization carries on. There are many different kinds; filing clerks, telephone order clerks, account clerks and so on.

Receptionists take care of visitors to the organization. They often combine this with the job of operating the switchboard.

Secretaries are personal assistants to managers and administrators. A good secretary will type the employer's letters, keep the filing system in order, deal with letters, organize appointments, make travel arrangements, and generally organize the manager's life.

It may help to look at an actual case. Let's suppose that MUSICUBE Ltd is a company that makes and sells a type of plastic box for holding musical cassettes. MUSICUBE will need not only a factory to make the cubes in but an office section to run the business from.

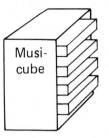

The product

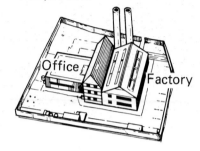

Office & Factory

MUSICUBE is doing well, and employs quite a few office staff. Let's pick out four of them and look at what their jobs involve:

JOHN JONES is the managing director of MUSICUBE.

He is the head of the board of directors which runs the company, and takes the final responsibility for all the decisions which are made. He is concerned with all aspects of the company's business, from what products to sell, how to market them and how much to charge customers, to the running of the factory and the office. It's a well paid job, but on the other hand if anything goes wrong anywhere in the company he has to take responsibility for it.

LUCY WALKER is the managing director's secretary.

She does everything she can to make his task of running the company easier. This means looking after his correspondence, handling his typing, keeping track of his appointments, managing his filing system, and generally looking after his day-to-day actions.

THELMA JAMES is the company accountant.

She is responsible – under the managing director – for the financial side of the company. She has her own clerical staff, who keep records of the money coming into the company from sale of goods and balance this against the money going out on rent, wages, raw materials and other expenses. The difference between money coming in and money going out is the profit, which everyone working for the company wants to make as large as possible!

JACK SMITH is a telephone order clerk dealing with sales.

He takes orders over the telephone for the company's goods; usually these orders are from shops wishing to stock musicubes. Mr Smith has to fill out an order form for each call, giving the details of the order. He will file one copy of this form, send another copy back to the customer to confirm the order, and pass a third copy through to the works so that production can be scheduled.

You'll notice that all these people spend a lot of time handling *information* of different kinds, a great deal of it on paper. For example, John Jones needs information on how well the company is doing to help him make decisions for the future; Thelma James needs information about what money is coming into the company and what money is going out of it; and so on. Most of the activities in an office involve passing information around; this will be important when we come to look at how machines can help with office work. Dealing with information in this way, whether by hand, using an office machine, or on a computer, is called *DATA PROCESSING* – DP for short.

Things to do

1 Make a list of all the local organizations you know of which you think would have an office section. Then put them into two columns: one for those concerned with selling goods or services to make a profit, the other for those which are simply concerned with getting a job done.

2 Here is a list of jobs which might be done in an office, and another of some common types of clerical staff. *In your workbook*, copy the diagram and draw lines connecting the jobs to the type of staff who would probably do them:

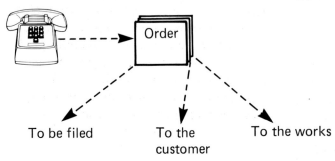

To be filed   To the customer   To the works

Taking an order on the
telephone and filling out an
order form

BOOK-KEEPERS

Adding up rows of figures
in a ledger

Altering the address on
a record holding a
customer's account

SHORTHAND
TYPISTS

Opening the managing
director's mail

CLERKS

Arranging an appointment
for a customer of the
business to call in and see a
director

Taking dictation   RECEPTIONISTS

Typing letters

Greeting visitors to the
office and arranging
for them to be taken to
the correct room   SECRETARIES

3 What kind of information do you think
that each of the types of staff given in
question 2 would have to deal with?

2 Office machines

Look at the photograph overleaf. It shows
an office, and one of the first things you'll
notice is that the office is full of machinery
of one type or another. These days office
machinery is so common that even the
smallest office is likely to have at least a
typewriter and a calculating machine. Yet
until the beginning of the twentieth
century, most offices contained no
machines at all. All records were kept by
hand, originally written with a quill pen
and then later on with a fountain pen.
Calculations were almost always done by
hand, which meant that many clerks had
to spend a great deal of time adding up
columns of figures.

Time has changed all that. This century
has seen the invention of a great many
different machines to make office work
easier. You already know that the
computer is one of these, and now is in
many ways the most important, but it
wasn't the first. Later in the chapter, we'll
be looking in detail at how computers
come into the picture, but let's start by
considering office machinery in general.
See if you can make a list of machines
(not computers) which you might find in
use an office – the picture overleaf will
start you off. You'll probably be surprised
at at how many you know when you put
your mind to it.

There are too many types of machine
involved to look at them all in detail, but
these are some of the most important
kinds:

1 Typewriters
The typewriter is one of the most useful
office machines ever invented. Although
they've been around for a good many
years now, the basic principles have
remained the same – putting in a piece of
paper and then pressing keys to produce
printed text on the paper. All kinds of
models are now available, from simple
manual typewriters to sophisticated
electric machines which can even come
supplied with memory like a computer.

Underwood Standard Typewriter No 5 – 1920

Busy modern office

2 Copying and duplicating machines

There are many different machines available to make copies of documents. Below is a picture of one type, which turns out multiple copies of carbon originals, you will probably have been given materials at school which were produced on one of these. The most common type of machine now being used in offices is the *photocopier*. These come in many different sizes, and can produce copies of documents quickly and fairly cheaply.

Banda duplicator

3 Microfiche readers

Paperwork in an office takes up a lot of space. One way of reducing this is to photograph documents and then to reduce their size on film. Small oblongs of film about the size of a postcard can each hold tiny pictures of a great number of sheets of paper. These pieces of film are called *microfiche*. They can be read using a microfiche reader, which enlarges the pictures again on to a screen. You may have seen this method being used in a local library to handle details about the books in circulation, or perhaps in a shop when you were ordering something.

4 Calculating machines

Machines of one sort or another have been used to help in office calculations for a very long time. Adding machines of the simplest kind can be used to help with additions and subtractions. Some produce paper 'listings' to be checked off afterwards if necessary. More complicated machines are available for other types of calculation, and all kinds of different pocket calculators can now be bought very cheaply indeed – these use the standard types of microprocessors described in chapter 4, and show just how cheap microprocessor-based products can become if enough of them are sold.

5 Accounting machines

These are special machines for keeping simple accounts. An accounting machine has a keyboard and a printing section in the same way as a mechanical adding machine, but it can do more processing – not just calculations, but

Library microfiche reader and operator

arranging and printing text – and it has simple program control built in so that not all instructions have to be entered at the keyboard.

6 Communications equipment

Offices need to receive and send messages. To do this, almost any office will have at least one telephone, and many will have a switchboard to allow incoming calls to be passed to any one of several phones. Another piece of communications equipment often in use is a teleprinter. This is a combination of a typewriter and a telephone, and is used to send and receive messages over long distances using a British Telecom system called *telex*.

These are just a few examples of the types of machine which can be found in offices. There are many others; we haven't even mentioned dictation machines, for example, or any of the different types of machine which can be used for sorting and handling post.

When computers first began to be found in offices, they were just another type of machine – useful, and new in design, but not revolutionary. Recent years, however, have seen a change since computers are now able to alter the whole way in which offices work. In the next section, we'll be looking at that change, and going back to what we've already learned about computers to try and understand what it is about them that makes them so important.

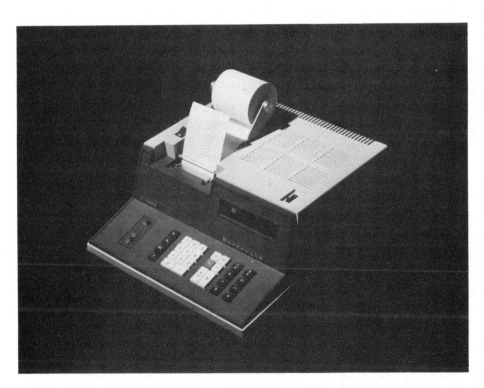

Burroughs C4300 accounting machine

67

Things to do

1 What kind of office machine would you expect to find doing each of the following jobs, and which type of office worker would be using it? (There may be more than one answer to both questions. Write them down *in your workbook*.)

JOB

Pricing an order

Making three copies of an incoming letter

Keeping accounts

Receiving a telephone call and linking it to an office phone

Storing dictation to be typed later

Typing a report

Making fifty copies of a typed report

Looking at records which have been reduced in size and then stored

Receiving a long-distance message in printed form

---

2 What office machines (if any) do you think that our four MUSICUBE staff would use, and to do what jobs? (Write down the answers *in your workbook*.)

MEMBER OF STAFF

John Jones
Lucy Walker
Thelma James
Jack Smith

---

3 Where does the computer come in?

The large, clumsy computers made in the 1940's would have been of no use in offices. They were far too big, they were always breaking down, and they could do little other than calculations. However during the 1950's computers moved out of the laboratories and into business, and people realised that this new type of machine could be a useful tool for more than just doing sums. As time went on, computers were used for more and more jobs in more and more places. We've already seen that modern computers are both cheap and powerful, as a result, they can be found everywhere from the home to the latest space rocket. Among the places where computers are making their mark, the office is one of the most important.

Why is this? What does the computer provide that helps office workers to do their jobs better? Go back to chapter 1 and see if you can suggest some answers to these questions; then look at the following list and see how many of these points you thought of.

Benefits of using computers in the office
a) Storage space
Any office, no matter how small, has to store information – things like names and addresses, personal details about people, prices, money owed, and so on. Office workers deal with a lot of this sort of information. The average office will contain many filing cabinets and cupboards, which hold great numbers of paper records. They take up a lot of space, and it often isn't easy to get at the one which is needed in a hurry, no matter how well they are filed.

Computer backing storage has two advantages over the use of paper records. First of all, it's *smaller*, which means that one cassette or floppy disc can hold a great deal of information. A floppy disc like the ones shown here can store the contents of a short book. Magnetic tapes can hold even more, and so can packs of 'hard discs' – these have several discs mounted together on a central spindle, rather like a cake stand.

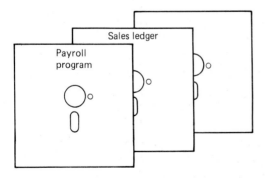

The other advantage computer storage gives over paper storage is the speed of access; that is, the time it takes to get a particular piece of information out of the system when it is needed. Computers can

access the information held on backing storage extremely quickly. On discs, the computer is able to go straight to the piece of information needed, in the same way as you can lift the stylus directly to the track you want when you are playing an LP. This is called *DIRECT ACCESS*. More time is needed when the information is stored on magnetic tape, as the records before the one you want have to be wound through first; this is similar to the process you have to go through if you want to play the last track on a musical cassette. This method of getting at information is called *SERIAL ACCESS*.

b) Processing
We already know that computers are very good at processing. Jobs such as totalling up rows of figures, checking totals with other totals, or rearranging lines in a letter take quite a while when they are done by hand. Using computers can speed things up.

c) Input and output
For an office computer to be useful, information must be input to it. This is generally the most time-consuming part of a computer system. However once the information is safely stored, there are many useful ways in which it can be output. For instance, stored information can often be accessed quickly and easily simply by typing in a request or an enquiry and waiting for the answer to be displayed on the screen.

d) Program control
Some types of job are necessary in almost every office. For example, any organization employing people will need to calculate their wages and produce payslips; every typist and secretary will be handling letters; any accounts clerk will be

adding up figures; and so on. Because other organizations too will be doing these things, it is possible to buy standard computer programs for many of them. Buying a program of this kind means that the office can have the advantage of the computer's speed at this kind of processing without the disadvantage of having to write instructions in a computer language.

e) Communications

Computers can be linked together using what are called *communications lines*. These are cables over which information can be sent for long distances (telephone lines are often used). It's possible for computers to 'talk' to one another over a distance simply by sending messages in this way, rather like two people using a phone.

As you can see, there are many ways in which computers can help office staff. Before we get too enthusiastic, however, we need also to look briefly at some of the problems. Computers are extremely useful, but they also have drawbacks, and it's important that we know what these are if we're going to end up with a balanced picture. Can you suggest any difficulties which you think the use of computers in an office might bring? Make your own list; then seen how many of the following points you thought of.

Problems of using computers

a) They break down.

These days, not very often, but it can happen. Engineers have to be brought in, and if there's something seriously wrong the work of the office can be disrupted.

b) They make mistakes.

In fact, the mistakes are almost always made by people – either the people putting in the information or the person who wrote the program of instructions – but computers have no common sense at all, and won't notice a mistake that might stand out very clearly if it were a person doing the processing. Stories are told of computers that have paid out vast cheques, or sent a final demand for the sum of £0.00p; this is usually due to some error in a program.

c) They lose information.

Unfortunately, magnetic media – discs and tapes – are very sensitive to things like heat, dust and humidity. When information is stored on a computer, at least one copy of it should always be kept somewhere else just in case something goes wrong.

d) They take away people's jobs.

There's a lot of argument going on about whether this is true or not. In chapter 8 we shall be looking at the whole question of how computers affect jobs. In the meantime, however, it's worth thinking back to what we said in chapter 1 – that computers can only do what they've been programmed to do. You, on the other hand, can cope with unexpected problems, you can deal sympathetically with other people, and can have spontaneous good ideas. Computers are bad at all these things. In many areas of work, there's just no substitute for the human touch.

Things to do

1 Work with a friend to try and answer the following questions about MUSICUBE Ltd:

a) What kind of information does the office section need to store on files? Can you suggest *five* examples?

b) What processing, if any, is carried out on each piece of information suggested in the answer to the last question?

c) Make a list of the types of message which you would expect MUSICUBE to be receiving from customers and other organizations. How would these messages be likely to arrive?

d) The managing director is thinking of buying a computer to help run the office systems. Advise him by making a list in your workbook of both the advantages that this could bring and the disadvantages that he would need to consider.

4 Computers in the office

Word processors

Have you ever used a typewriter? If so, you'll know how easily mistakes are made. Beginners make a good many, and even a well-trained typist or secretary will sometimes hit the wrong key.

Suppose that MUSICUBE wanted to send a letter to its customers advertising its product. Part of the letter might read like a) below.

The whole letter would be given to a typist to produce. It might be typed correctly the first time, copied, and it could then be sent out to the customers. However there could be problems, either because the person doing it makes a typing error or because the employer then decides that the letter must be changed in some way.

Here is a list of some of the things which might go wrong:

1 The typist makes a spelling mistake; for instance, putting DEAR CUSTOMOR

2 The typist leaves out a character; for instance, DEAR CUSTOMR,

3 An extra line has to be inserted, so that the letter reads as in b) below.

4 Each letter has to be personalised; that is, it must start DEAR MS SMITH, or whatever the customer's name is, instead of simply DEAR CUSTOMER.

If the letter has been produced on a typewriter, these kinds of change are difficult to make. It is not easy to delete characters and whole words, and even more difficult to put in extra material, or to produce personalised copies of a letter without having to retype the whole thing.

a)
```
DEAR CUSTOMER,


WE'D LIKE TO TELL YOU ABOUT OUR NEW RANGE OF MUSICUBES AND
GIVE YOU THE OPPORTUNITY TO ORDER THEM AT SPECIAL RATES.
```

b)
```
DEAR CUSTOMER,


THIS IS A PERSONAL MESSAGE FROM MUSICUBE LTD. WE'D LIKE TO
TELL YOU ABOUT OUR NEW RANGE OF MUSICUBES AND GIVE YOU THE
OPPORTUNITY TO ORDER THEM AT SPECIAL RATES.
```

To help typists with this sort of problem, electronic typewriters are now available which have many of the features of a computer.

Now that computer systems are so cheap, however, it is possible to go even further than that and install in your office a type of computer which has been specially designed to handle text. These are called *WORD PROCESSORS*. You can see a photograph of one opposite.

Using a word processor instead of a typewriter, it doesn't matter if the operator makes mistakes or needs to put in extra lines. When the operator types in a letter, it is held in the computer's memory in the same way as a program is held when you are working on it. If there is a mistake in the typing, it can be corrected. Once the letter is correct, the typist stores it on disc. It can then be called up for any changes to it, or the computer can be given an instruction to print a copy on the printer.

Go back to the list of things which might go wrong when typing a letter, and see how easy it would be to cope with these problems if you were using a word processor rather than a typewriter. This is why word processors are becoming increasingly popular in offices.

For most computers it is possible to buy a word processing program or set of programs. When one of these is running, the computer will act as a specialised word processor, handling, storing and printing text. There is probably a program like this available on your computer so that you can try out this kind of facility.

Business systems

We've already said that most of the work which goes on in offices is concerned with handling information of some sort. This information used to be held on paper, but these days much of it is stored on computer. The computer is then able to process the information into whatever form is needed.

Let's go back to MUSICUBE. As a medium-sized company which has been running for some years and is profitable, MUSICUBE has been able to computerise quite a lot of the work which goes on in its office. To do this, it uses a minicomputer.

All organizations like MUSICUBE, involved in manufacturing goods and then selling them, will work in roughly the same way. This is because the same jobs have to be done whatever the company or the line of business it is engaged in. For instance, MUSICUBE will need a *PAYROLL* system, to give staff their wages. It will need a *SALES* department, to deal with selling products to customers. It will have an *ACCOUNTS* department, to keep track of the company's money. It will need a *PURCHASING* system, to buy in the raw materials it uses to manufacture musicubes. And so on.

These are called BUSINESS SYSTEMS. They are needed to run the company. MUSICUBE has transferred all its important business systems to the minicomputer. Let's look at two of them to see how this works:

1 The PAYROLL system
MUSICUBE employees are paid for their work in different ways. Some of the workforce are weekly paid; they receive a pay packet holding their wages in cash. Most of the factory workers are paid by this system, and also some of the junior clerical staff in the office.

Other staff are on monthly salaries.

IBM electronic typewriter 75

Handling text on an ICL word processing system

These staff either have their money paid directly into their bank accounts, or they are given a cheque for the amount each month. Directors and managers are all salaried, and so are most of the office staff.

The computer is used to work out how much money to pay each worker. This is a complicated calculation, because a great many different things have to be taken into account. Do you know what different factors the computer would have to know about and allow for if it was calculating how much to put into a weekly paid worker's pay packet? See if you can make a list; then compare it with the one below.

Needed to calculate wages

a) Number of basic hours worked

b) Rate per basic hour

c) Number of overtime hours worked

d) Rate per overtime hour

e) Sick pay

f) Holiday pay

g) National Insurance due

h) Income tax due

i) Pension due

Why does MUSICUBE run its payroll on computer rather than doing it by hand or on some other machine? There are four main reasons:

1 *STORAGE* – the computer is able to hold the details about rates of tax and national insurance, pay scales, what every worker has already earned, and so on.

This saves the clerks having to check them every week.

2 *SPEED* – working out pay involves a lot of complicated calculations which the computer is very fast and accurate at doing.

3 *OUTPUT* – the computer is able to print pay slips to go with the pay packet

4 *CHEAPNESS* – all companies have to work out pay in the same way. Because of this, MUSICUBE hasn't had to go to the expense of writing its own programs to run the payroll system; it has been able to buy ready-written programs.

2 The order processing system

Orders come into MUSICUBE in two different ways. Most arrive by telephone and are written down by Jack Smith and his colleagues. The rest are sent in through the post.

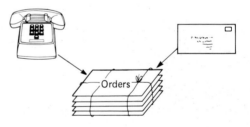

Once orders have arrived, clerical staff type them into the computer via a VDU screen and keyboard. The computer program which deals with the order entry is able to make checks on the orders to try to stop mistakes being processed. For instance, it looks up the details of the customer making the order to make sure that he or she doesn't already owe too much money; it checks that the order isn't too short or too long; it makes sure that the products wanted are still available; and so on. If the order passes all these tests, the computer can then help in another way. Details of the company's prices are held on file, so the computer program can access them and put the price against each line of the order.

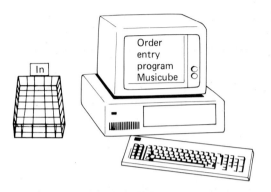

Once the orders have been accepted and priced, three-part copies are printed: one to be stored, one to be returned to the customer, and a third to go to the works.

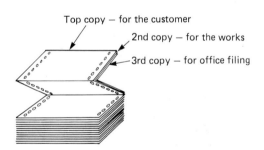

Top copy – for the customer

2nd copy – for the works

3rd copy – for office filing

The computer's work doesn't end there. It helps in other ways. At the end of each week, it processes the week's orders and produces a schedule for what is being made in the works. When orders are ready to go out, delivery notes are printed to send with them. After the delivery has been made, the computer program prints an invoice to send out to the customer.

MUSICUBE wasn't able to buy in standard software for its order processing system; it had to employ staff to write programs specially for it. It feels that it was worth it, however, since the computer

system helps to process orders accurately, efficiently, and above all, fast!

There are a great many different uses for computers in office work; in this chapter, we have only been able to mention a few of them. As computer systems become cheaper and more powerful, further ways are being found in which they can benefit the office worker. Some of these will be looked at in more detail in the next chapter, which is concerned with recent advances in types of computer system which can be found at work.

To finish this chapter, however, let's look briefly at an idea which sounds as though it's out of a science fiction novel but which might one day become reality. If you have watched any television programs on computers, you may have heard of something called 'the electronic office'.

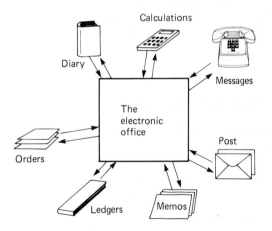

The idea behind this is to put almost every piece of information in the office – coming in, being stored, or going out – on computer. Different computer systems in the office would be linked together, and paper would become virtually a thing of the past.

Messages, for instance, would be handled by a computer. It would deal with the switchboard, act as an automatic answering machine, and store incoming messages on personal computer files.

Diaries of appointments would also be held on file, and kept up to date by a computer.

Text – letters, reports and so on – would all be handled by word processing software.

Business information would be handled and processed as computerised data,. . . . and so on.

Some of these ideas are already being tried out, but at the moment it looks as though the day when the average office becomes totally computerised is still in the future. However things move so fast in the computer world that predictions are difficult to make. It would be interesting to be able to see into the future and find out how many of these ideas became realities!

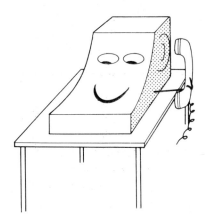

Things to do

1 If you have a word processing program available on your microcomputer, use it to type in a letter like the one mentioned on page 71. When you have completed this, change some of the lines to read differently (you could address the letter to somewhere different, or alter the sense of what it says). Finally, file the letter on backing storage and instruct the computer to print a copy on the printer.

2 Draw a diagram of a typical word processing system, showing the different devices and their links to one another.

3 Explain the difference between weekly paid staff and salaried staff. List *three* reasons why payrolls are usually run on computer.

4 Suppose you were given the choice of working in an office with a great many computer systems or one without. State which you would prefer, and give *three* reasons for your choice.

6

The new technology

What will this chapter teach you?

This chapter looks at some of the more recent developments in computing and how they make the computer an increasingly powerful tool in a variety of different workplaces.

You will be **exploring** the following areas:

1 the nature and use of computer graphics;

2 making computer models of real situations;

3 using computers to help in decision-making;

4 methods of processing data;

5 computerised banks of data;

6 buying software off-the-shelf.

1 Computer graphics

What are they?

In the last few chapters, we've looked in some detail at ways in which computers can handle numbers and text. However this isn't the whole story. In recent years, computer systems have been developed which are also very good at dealing with pictures. Computer facilities of this kind are called *COMPUTER GRAPHICS*.

Almost certainly, you will already have made use of some computer graphics.

Have you ever played Space Invaders, Pacman or any other of the popular computer games? These are examples of computer graphics in action.

How do they work?

There isn't a standard way to program a computer to draw pictures. Generally, there are different instructions for different machines. Most modern microcomputers have good graphics facilities. Let's look briefly at the BBC micro and the kind of pictures that can be produced using the BBC graphics instructions.

It is very easy to program the BBC micro to draw pictures. Using special graphics instructions in the BASIC language, the programmer is able to *draw* on the VDU screen, in lines and dots, use different *colours* for the picture, and even instruct the computer to make *sounds*, through a built-in loudspeaker.

Let's look at an example. The program below illustrates some of the instructions in use. If you have a BBC micro, key it in and run it.

```
 10 MODE 5
 20 GCOL 0,130
 30 GCOL 0,1
 40 CLG
 50 MOVE 100,100
 60 DRAW 100,500
 70 DRAW 500,500
 80 DRAW 500,100
 90 DRAW 100,100
100 SOUND 1,-6,53,20
110 SOUND1,-6,65,20
120 SOUND 1,-6,73,20
```

The program first goes into a special graphics 'mode', which allows it to draw pictures. It then turns the VDU screen yellow, draws a red square on it, and plays three notes. Look at the program again. Can you work out which instruction is responsible for each of these actions?

More expensive computers have still more graphics facilities available. One type of input device called a *GRAPHICS TABLET*. These allow pictures to be drawn by hand and then stored in computer memory.

As well as input devices for graphics, there are also output devices. You've already seen that the VDU screen is one of these; another can be seen below. It's called a *GRAPHICS PLOTTER*, and can produce a drawing of graphic information stored on the computer.

Hewlett-Packard Model 7225A Graphics Plotter

What are they used for?

We've already mentioned that graphics are used for computer games. Although these are mainly for fun, some also have serious uses; for instance, educational games exist to help people learn about anything from simple mathematics to making business decisions.

But computer graphics have other uses, too. They can be of help to anyone whose work involves pictures. Artists, for instance, can build up their ideas in a computer. This is particularly useful to cartoon animators, who have to draw many thousands of pictures, each one only varying from the one before in tiny details. Storing the drawings on a computer makes it very easy to make minor changes to them. *Designers* also find that computer graphics can be of help in their work. We'll be looking at some examples of this in the next chapter. As computers with graphics facilities become cheaper and more powerful, it is likely that more and more uses will be found for this particular aspect of computer processing.

Things to do

1 Suggest *three* uses for computer graphics.

2 Name *one* graphics input device and one graphics output device.

3 If you have a BBC microcomputer, alter the program given so that the VDU turns green, not red, and a triangle, not a square, is drawn (you will need to consult the BBC user manual to find out how to do this).

2 Modelling with computers

Making models is a common activity. Many people – adults and children – make models as a hobby, out of everything from plasticine and clay to matchsticks.

This kind of model is generally made for pleasure. However, there are also models which have a more serious purpose and are used to help people in their jobs. Some of these are simply physical mock-ups of how the finished thing should look. An architect, for instant, designing a new house, might use a scale model to show how the final house would appear. But not every model needs to look like the thing which it represents; it is often enough if it simply *behaves* like it. A company accountant might make a financial model of the organization which wouldn't look at all like the company, since it would only be a collection of figures, but which would behave in the same way as the real company when changes are made to part of it.

This kind of modelling – trying to construct something which *behaves* like the real thing rather than *looking* like it – can be very helpful in a great many different professions. A theoretical model of this kind can be built up on a computer, where it is often referred to as a *SIMULATION*.

Let's look at a very simple example of a simulation program (see overleaf). Suppose that we want to write a computer program to simulate the behaviour of a slot machine which dispenses stamps. Three types of stamps are available from this machine. Red ones cost 10p, green ones cost 20p and blue ones cost 30p. To buy a stamp, it is necessary to put in the exact money and then press a go button; the stamp is then produced.

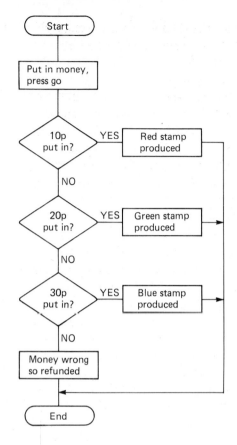

We can draw a flowchart to show the way in which this machine behaves.

Using the same logical structure, we can write a BASIC program to simulate the behaviour of this machine.

Notice that the computer you use to run this program won't look like the slot machine, and it won't take money or give stamps. What it will do is tell you how the machine would behave if you were to try putting certain sums of money in. There are many things it *can't* tell us about the machine's behaviour; for instance, what would happen if instead of putting money in it we attacked the machine with an axe. This is typical of simulation programs, which can't generally give a complete picture of whatever they are simulating, only a simplified version.

The use of computer graphics can make programs of this kind far more effective than they were previously. For instance, graphics could be added to the program above to show what the machine would actually do rather than just explaining it. Many of the popular computer games are simple simulations centred around use of graphics, based on such activities as finding a way through a maze or landing a space ship on the moon.

```
10 PRINT "HOW MANY PENCE DO YOU WANT TO PUT IN ?"
20 INPUT A
30 IF A=10 THEN PRINT "YOU HAVE BOUGHT A RED STAMP":GOTO 80
40 IF A=20 THEN PRINT "YOU HAVE BOUGHT A GREEN STAMP":GOTO 80
50 IF A=30 THEN PRINT "YOU HAVE BOUGHT A BLUE STAMP":GOTO 80
60 PRINT "WRONG MONEY-COINS REFUNDED"
70 GOTO 10
80 END
```

We've looked at a very simple example of a modelling program. In practice, programs of this kind are usually extremely complicated to write, since programming a computer with patterns of behaviour is a difficult task. Simulations are useful in many areas of work. A well-known example is the use of computer simulation to train pilots in flying skills. The photograph below shows a session in progress.

Using computer simulations is a way of trying out things safely and cheaply. Once a model has been built up within a computer, it is possible to experiment with the effects of making different decisions simply by varying the input to the program. To understand why this is useful, you have only to imagine what the effects might be if, for instance, we trained our airline pilots by immediately putting them in planes and letting them see what they could do!

Things to do

1 Suggest simulation programs which each of the following people would find useful:

a) an astronaut;

b) an industrial chemist;

c) a car designer;

d) a military commander.

2 Suggest ways in which computer graphics could be used to improve the effectiveness of the slot machine program given in this section.

3 Decision-making

All of us spend a great deal of our time making decisions. They can range in importance from the everyday decision of what to have for breakfast all the way to military decisions which may mean the difference between victory and defeat.

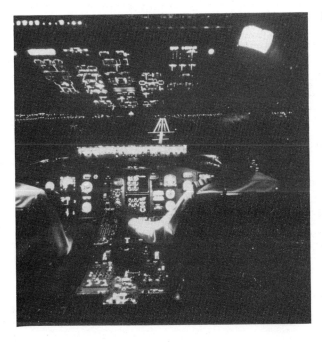

British Airways 757 pilot simulator

Taking decisions is a part of everyone's life. In particular, it's a part of people's jobs. Even the simplest job will involve moments when it's necessary to choose a way to do something, and being promoted at work generally means starting to take more important decisions. The manager, considering the most profitable course of action for the company, is having to take many decisions. So is the lawyer who is choosing the best way to present a client's case. Doctors make decisions about illnesses and the best methods of treating them; and a politician's whole job is about taking decisions on running the country.

Where does the computer come into this? Well, we've already seen in chapter 3 how computers can be programmed to take decisions in their own right. They can also be invaluable aids to the decision – maker by providing information which will help him to make up his mind. Let's look at some examples of this.

First, a game. The BBC computer Welcome tape includes a program called KINGDOM (there are similar games available on many other micros). KINGDOM, when run, invites the player to take a number of decisions concerning the running of a small village – how much rice to keep each year for seed, how the labour force should be divided between planting in the fields and protecting the village, and so on. Then the program simulates putting these decisions into action within the village and tells you how well you've managed to keep it running. The beginner usually finds that he's ended up starving the entire population of the village to death, or made some other disastrous mistake. As he continues to play, however, he learns which decisions are unwise, and his performance improves.

Of course, it's only a game. But it's not so far from reality. Take our next example. Exactly the same principle as this is used when the Chancellor of the Exchequer is preparing the annual Budget. His job is to propose the right measures to balance the economy and have the other effects which he wants. To help him do this, he has a team of highly qualified people, but he also has the services of a large computer. This contains a computer model of the economy, into which the proposed Budget measures can be fed. When the program is run, it simulates the effect of the measures on the economy, and the results are used to help guide the Chancellor in his final choice. The system is a long way from perfect – the economy is too complicated to model completely, the computer holds only a simplified version – but this provides the Chancellor with a powerful tool to help him in getting it right.

Business managers, too, take many decisions. These are generally concerned with the most efficent and profitable running of their companies. Here, the computer has a major role to play as a provider of information. A good 'management information system', as this type of system is called, will be able to give the manager much invaluable analysis on such matters as the most profitable products and branches, and also to help in future planning. With a tool this powerful to assist, the manager is able to come to well-informed decisions rather than make shrewd guesses.

Finally, let's look at a doctor. Her decisions are particularly important, since they can literally involve life or death. The first decision that she generally has to make about any patient will be her diagnosis of his complaint; in other words, she needs to say what's wrong with him. If she makes a mistake at this stage, the consequences can be tragic.

One of the tools now available to help the doctor is a program which is able to make a diagnosis itself. It works like this. First, the patient is asked a series of questions about his or her symptoms, and examined in the normal way (no, not by

Houses of Parliament

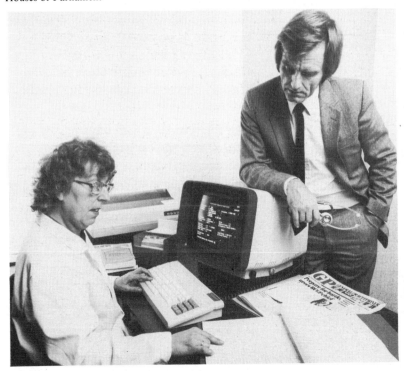

Computer use in the medical profession

the computer!). Then the results are fed into the computer, and it is able to look up all the possible complaints which are stored in its large memory and match these with the symptoms to suggest the most likely ones. A computer system which is able to give professional advice in this way is known as an *EXPERT SYSTEM*. A program of this kind is able not only to give advice – which is all that it is used for in the delicate area of medicine – but to take decisions on its own, on the basis of the rules programmed and the store of information which it holds. If this type of system becomes widespread in our society, it could have far-reaching consequences on the way we think and work.

Things to do

1 Suggest decisions that you think each of the following jobs involves making:

   a) bartender

   b) footballer

   c) geologist

   d) navigator

   e) judge

   In how many of these cases could a computer system provide help in making the decisions? What form should such help take?

2 Mr Howard is the owner and manager of a high street shop, which he runs as a video-hire business. He has been advised that he could use a small computer system to help him run the business more efficently and profitably.

   Suggest ways in which such a system would help him to make better business decisions.

4 Types of processing

For many years, computers used in business have worked in a mode called *BATCH PROCESSING*. This meant running data through a computer system in groups of records called *BATCHES*.

To show you how this method of processing works, let's suppose that we want to put twenty records holding names and addresses into a computer and store them on a file. Using batch processing techniques, it could be done like this:

a) The paper records are converted into a machine-readable form (this is usually PUNCHED CARDS, special cards which hold data in the form of holes punched in them).

b) The data on the punched cards is then input to the computer system through a card-reader.

c) A computer program checks that the information which has been input is as accurate as possible (this is called *VALIDATION*, and is a very important part of any input program) and produces a report, on the printer, to show which records failed the tests.

d) All the records which have passed are stored in a file on backing storage – often on a reel of magnetic tape.

This type of system works well, and is used for many commercial computer applications. However, in recent years a different way of processing has come into general use, mainly centred around the use of VDU's linked to a computer. This technique is called *ON-LINE PROCESSING*, because it involves sending information to and from a computer down a communications line. In on-line systems, records are usually dealt with one by one, not in a batch. Let's go back to our twenty records and look at an on-line method of processing them. It could be done in the following way:

a) Each record is typed in at a keyboard with a formatted screen – a VDU – where it is passed down the line to the central computer.

b) The record is validated *immediately* by a computer program (if you think back to chapter 3, *you've* written a program involving instant validation of input) and a message showing whether it has been accepted or rejected is shown on the screen.

c) If the record is valid, it is put on file on backing storage – probably on some type of magnetic disc.

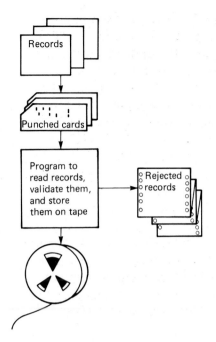

Batch processing

The main advantage of using an on-line system is in saving time. There is almost no delay in finding out errors in the input data, unlike batch processing systems where you have to wait until the program has finished running and then consult the printed report.

On-line systems are also pleasant to use, and are becoming increasingly popular. They are particularly useful when it is necessary to make enquiries about information held on a computer file, or to alter it quickly. When an on-line system is able to change or add information to a file immediately, like the one described above, it is called a *REAL-TIME* system. If you have ever booked a ticket on an aeroplane, you will have used a system like the one on page 86; your reservation will have been sent in via a VDU and will have instantly been used to change the details which are held on file about seats on that flight.

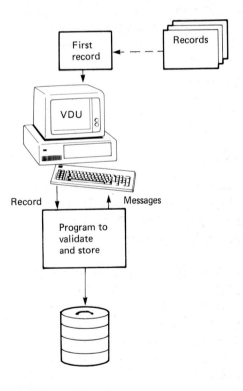

On-line processing

Thomas Cook – travel agents – booking tickets through a real-time system

We have said that VDU's are the main input devices used in on-line systems; however they are not the only ones. Let's look at a different method of input which will shortly be coming into common use. You will probably have noticed that recently goods bought in supermarkets have started to carry a special strip, like the one shown in the photograph opposite. These are called *BAR CODES*. The stripes represent letters and numbers, but in machine-readable form. Special readers are being installed at supermarket checkouts, so that when you buy an item the assistant is able to put the details of it into a computer simply by passing a type of wand over the code. This will speed up the checking out process by helping both

the customer and the store, and also means that a record of the company's stock and how much has been sold can be held on computer storage. Bar codes have many uses; you may also have come across them being used as input to your local library system.

Things to do

1 Put TRUE or FALSE *in your workbooks* against each of the following statements:

a) It is best to use a *batch processing* system if you expect to make frequent enquires about the information held on it.

b) *Validation* means checking data to make sure that it is accurate.

c) The most common method of entering data into *on-line* systems is by means of punched cards.

d) *Real-time* systems process data in batches.

e) Airline ticket booking systems are usually *real-time*.

2 Check to see how many things you can find in your house which have bar codes on the wrappings. The kitchen is a good place to start, but it's not the only place. When you've done this, see if you can work out from the results which stores are putting these codes on their goods. Visit the stores concerned, and see if any of them are using special bar code readers at the checkout yet.

5 Collections of data

If you wanted to catch a bus or train into town, but didn't have a timetable, how would you find out what services ran?

Well, you might have a timetable which you picked up last time you had this problem; but it would be old now, and perhaps out of date. You could try phoning up the station; but when you do that the line could be engaged or nobody will answer the call. Or you could do it the energetic way, by going to the station on

IBM 3660 Supermarket System – high speed optical scanner

foot to find out, but that would take you a long time, since it's three miles away.

The quickest and surest method would be for all the information about the routes and fares to be stored on a computer, with software and communication lines allowing it to be easily accessed. Then, if you had a VDU in your home which was on-line to the computer, your problem would be solved. All you would need to do to find out about buses and trains would be to type in an enquiry and wait for the answer to be displayed on the screen. Simple, and you wouldn't need to worry about whether your information was out of date, since the computer system would be kept supplied with details of all changes to services.

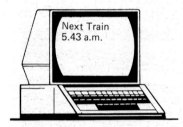

This may sound far-fetched, but it's not – systems of this sort are available. Modern computers are extremely good at holding large quantities of data and providing ways for it to be accessed quickly. Collections of data which are specially designed to allow people to get at them easily are called *DATABASES*. Here are just a few of the situations in which a database might be used:

a) in a library, to hold details of all the books in stock and allow people to make enquiries about particular books or subjects,

b) in a large company, to hold information about the company's performance in order to help management in making decisions,

c) in a manufacturing company, to hold details about the products which are designed and made there,

d) in a school or college, to hold student records giving name, address and other information so that student details can be quickly accessed.

These are all examples of databases, which would be used by the particular organization which holds its information on them. They depend not only on a lot of memory space but on very carefully structured programs to hold and access the data so that it can be obtained from the system as quickly and efficently as possible.

A database of this kind, however, would still not solve your problem about train times. What's needed for that is a public database; a collection of data which anyone who wants to know about train times is able to get at. Systems which provide this kind of service are now available. They're called *DATABANKS*. Let's look at one of the most well-known of these and see how it works.

PRESTEL
PRESTEL is the trade name of a well-known databank service. It is based around a large computer which holds information of many different kinds. For example there might be details of local restaurants, paid for by an association of them which hopes that this will help trade; British Rail may hold its timetables on the service; weather reports might be available; and so on. Almost anything can be made available, the only important points are that someone is willing to

provide the information and that someone else wants to access it.

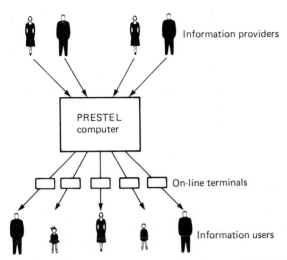

Information providers

PRESTEL computer

On-line terminals

Information users

If you want to receive PRESTEL information, you will need to buy or rent special equipment. PRESTEL terminals are available, or some microcomputers can be adapted to act as receivers. The information is sent out over the telephone network. Systems that use this network to transmit messages are known as *Viewdata*. On the other hand CEEFAX and ORACLE are databank systems that operate in a different way; they send their information to television sets, using a part of the television signal. Systems like this are known as *Teletext*. Although Viewdata and Teletext send signals in different ways, the service which they provide is similar.

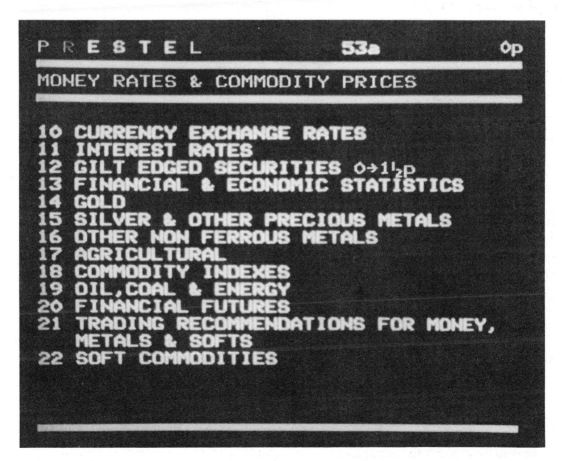

A screen of PRESTEL information

Things to do

1 If you visit a local television dealers, you should be able to obtain leaflets about PRESTEL or one of the other databank systems. Use these and any other information you are able to find to answer the following questions:

a) Do databanks of this kind work by batch processing or by on-line processing?

b) If you wished to use one of these services, how would you go about it?

c) How much would the service cost you?

d) What information would be available on the databank?

2 Suppose that you are asked to advise the chairman of British Rail about whether he should pay to have detailed rail timetables held on a databank service. List the advantages this would bring for him and the disadvantages you would need to warn him about.

6 Off-the-shelf software

We've already looked at programs in chapter 3, and you've tried writing a simple program yourself. One difficulty about computer programs, however, is that it can take a very long time to write them and test that they are working properly. Because of this, software is often the most expensive part of a computer system.

One way to get round this problem is to buy what are called *PACKAGES*. These are general-purpose programs which can be bought from a supplier of software. They are often called *off-the-shelf*

programs because it is intended that they can simply be bought, loaded and run. Although it's not always quite as simple as that, it is generally much cheaper to buy packaged software than to pay people to write special programs for you.

There are packages available for many standard jobs. We've already seen in chapter 5 how this type of program can be bought to run a payroll, and in fact financial systems like this are very often 'bought-in' in this way. Another area of work in which packages are frequently found is in the educational system, where schools and colleges use a number of standardised learning programs. Packages are so common that there's hardly an area of computing where they're not used. Although they'll never be able to answer all needs – there will always be applications which need special custom-written software – they have an important role to play in helping bring down the cost of computer software to a reasonable level.

Things to do

1 Give *three* examples of packaged software that you have come across, and explain what each one does and why it is a package rather than custom-written.

7 Information technology

Information technology is a general term

to cover all the ways in which we handle information. That doesn't just mean computers – although they're an important part of it – the term also covers micro-chips, television, telecommunications, electronic mail and so on. All these areas of technology are becoming so related to one another that it's useful to have a general term which means the whole range.

In a sense, this whole book is about information technology. Since it's a recent term, however, it's often associated most with the very newest technological developments, where such areas as telecommunications and on-line systems come together. The kind of systems we've been looking at in this chapter have involved some of these areas.

7

Industrial control

What will this chapter teach you?

This chapter continues our look at computers in working life, this time considering some of the qualities of the computer which make it a valuable tool in industry. We will be seeing how computers can be used for measuring and for controlling other machines and processes, and how these abilities can be used to help in the manufacture of goods.

You will be doing the following:

1 **learning** how computers can be used in the fields of control and measurement;

2 **finding out** the difference between analogue and digital devices;

3 **looking at** some examples of using a computer for control and measurement by seeing how simple devices can be linked up to a BBC microcomputer;

4 **extending** these ideas to show how computers can operate in industry, both in the design office and on the shop floor.

1 Controlling and measuring

In the last two chapters we've been looking at how computers affect the world of work, first in the office and then more generally. We've considered both office technology such as the word processor, and more general areas of information technology such as databanks and computer graphics.

This chapter also looks at how computers affect the workplace, but with a different slant. We'll be concerned now with ways in which computer technology can be useful in industrial processing. This will involve different types of systems, and we'll be looking more at the power of the computer to *control* and *measure* than at its data processing capabilities. Our main interest will be in microcomputers and microprocessors, since these are the type of computer most often found doing these jobs.

Using devices

Before we consider how computers can control machines or parts of machines, we need to find out something about the nature of the machines themselves.

We will refer to a machine or part of a machine as a *DEVICE*. Some examples of devices are switches, lamps, heaters, motors, sensors for touch and light, thermostats, thermometers and scales. Can you add to this list from your own knowledge?

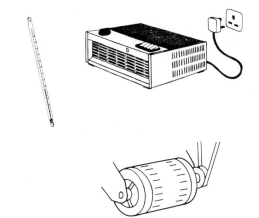

Modern machines are largely made up of devices like these. We want to explore how a computer can *control* these devices and use them for *measuring*.

Let's look at a washing machine. What devices would it contain? Try sketching one in your workbook and labelling the devices.

Many washing machines are now controlled by a built-in microprocessor. One of these machines might follow a program of instructions like the one below.

If we think carefully about the process which is going on there, we can see that at times the microprocessor is *controlling* switches and motors and at other times it is *measuring* time, temperature or water level.

For instance, a) is a control activity, c) is a measuring activity and b) is a mixture of measuring and control.

a)	The control switch starts the machine filling with hot and cold water.
b)	After *either* a certain time has passed *or* a certain level is reached, the control switch will stop the water coming.
c)	The temperature of the water is checked, using a form of thermometer.
d)	If the temperature is too low, the control switch starts the water heating until it is at the correct temperature.
e)	The control switch starts the motor which turns the drum holding the washing.
f)	After a certain time has passed, the control switch will stop the drum.
g)	The control switch will pump the dirty water out through the waste pipe.
h)	When the water level reaches zero, the control switch starts to fill the machine with cold water for the rinse.
i)	After *either* a certain time has passed *or* a certain level is reached, the control switch will stop the water coming.
j)	The control switch starts the motor to turn the drum, ...and so on

See if you can copy and complete this table by deciding which of the other activities is measuring, control or both. **(Do not mark this book.)**

CONTROL	MEASURING	BOTH
a	c	b
.	.	.
.	.	.
.	.	.
.	.	.

When a control activity is taking place, a message is being *sent* to the device. When a measuring activity is taking place, a message is being *received* from the device. A mixed activity means that the microprocessor is both *sending* messages to the device and *receiving* messages back from it.

The following diagrams show how this works:

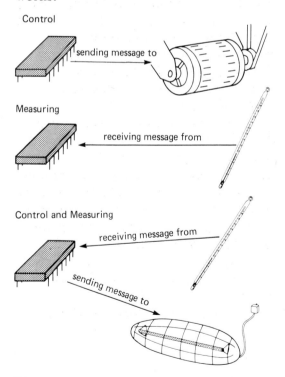

Control

sending message to

Measuring

receiving message from

Control and Measuring

receiving message from

sending message to

You can see that control means that the microprocessor is *outputting* electronic information to the device, measurement means that it is *inputting* information, and when it is doing both at once it is concerned with both *input and output*.

When a computer or microprocessor is receiving messages from a device and sending messages to it, there is a language problem. The microprocessor communicates by using a particular kind of electronic signal. Usually, however, the device doesn't talk the same language as the microprocessor. Because of this, something is needed to convert the signals from the microprocessor into a form which can directly control the device, and to convert the messages coming back from the device into the computer's electronic language, in the same way as an interpreter is needed when two people who speak different languages want to talk to one another.

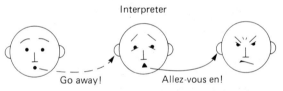

Interpreter

Go away!   Allez-vous en!

To solve this problem, an *INTERFACE* is required. This is the name given to the part of a computer which can do the translation.

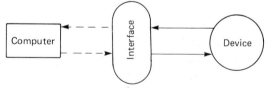

Computer   Interface   Device

All sizes of computers can be used to control and measure: main-frames, minis and micros. As well as this, microprocessors are particularly useful for this kind of function. As we saw in chapter 4, a microprocessor isn't very different from a very small computer.

In business data processing, a microprocessor on its own isn't a great deal of use because it can't store much information and it doesn't have very good methods of input and output. For control and measuring purposes, however, there isn't usually much information to be stored, and input and output take the form of electrical signals rather than printing on paper. Because of this, microprocessors are widely used for control and measuring. They are often built into machines, and act as small computers in the way that they work.

The number of possible uses for computer control and measuring is almost endless. Here are a few suggestions. Can you think of any more?

a) Controlling a central heating system in a factory, house or other building.

b) Measuring and controlling the operation of a car engine (can you think of any makes of car which have this facility built-in?)

c) Controlling a chemical process in a factory by keeping measurements of what is happening and taking any actions which are necessary; for example, when brewing beer.

Things to do

1 Continue the sequence of steps in programming a washing machine to include draining and spinning and a warning light which operates when the water gets too hot. Classify these activities into control, measuring and mixed.

2 List the main devices which you think would be found in:

a) an electric cooker;

b) a machine for brewing beer;

c) a greenhouse.

3 Draw up a sequence of activities for the operation of a central heating system heating two rooms with a thermostat in each room. Classify the activities into control, measuring and mixed.

2 Analogue and digital devices

We've already talked about devices such as thermometers, lights and switches; now we need to look more closely at their way of working. These devices fall into two categories; they are either *DIGITAL* or *ANALOGUE*.

Probably the most well known digital device is the digital watch.

The display on this kind of watch works in hours and minutes. It will continue to read 2:41 until a full minute is up, when the display will change to 2:42 by a sudden jump. Compare this with the old-fashioned type of watch. Here there are no sudden jumps. The hands creep smoothly round the face. This is an *analogue* device.

Considering these two types of watch shows us the difference between a digital and an analogue device. A *digital* device works in steps, by jumping from one step to another. The steps are always the same value; in the watch we have just looked at, for example, they were each one minute long. An *analogue* device, on the other hand, operates smoothly, not in steps; so the watch hands move smoothly, not jerkily.

Let's look at other examples of this.

1 Clinical thermometer

This is another analogue device. The mercury in it will rise smoothly to show the temperature reached.

2 Parking meter

Money is inserted into one of these in set amounts, and the time bought increases in a number of steps.

Computers of the kind we have been looking at in this book are all digital devices. Their circuitry processes information in *BINARY* form – that is, in noughts and ones, which can be counted as steps – rather than in analogue form. Microprocessors work in the same way.

If a computer is to be able to deal with input and output from all types of device, it will need to be able to handle both digital and analogue messages. One of the purposes of the *interface* is to make this possible. Even microcomputers, the smallest type of computer, generally have such an interface or can have special interface boards attached to them.

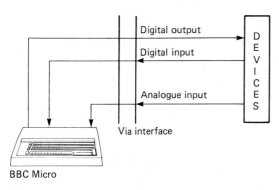

BBC Micro

Things to do

1 Copy and complete *in your workbook* the following table, classifying the following devices into analogue or digital:

Device		Analogue	Digital
a)	Thermometer	√	
b)	Electric cooker control knob		√
c)	Light switch		
d)	Volume switch on radio		
e)	Breathalyser (crystal kind)		
f)	Brake pedal on a car		
g)	Electric clock with second hand		
h)	Weighing machine with dial		
i)	Servo motor		
j)	Stepping motor		
k)	Abacus		
l)	Sliderule		
m)	Gear lever		

3 Some examples of microelectronic control and measuring

1 Traffic lights

Below is a diagram of a set of computerised traffic lights which count the cars going through them:

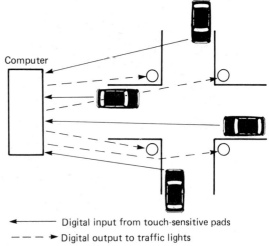

Computer

——— Digital input from touch-sensitive pads

– – – ▸ Digital output to traffic lights

This is an example of digital measurement, since the cars are counted one by one as they cross a touch-sensitive pad in the road. A computer program then produces digital output to set the lights accordingly.

We have not yet looked at programming for control and measurement situations. Until recently this was usually carried out by specialists who programmed in very technical languages, but micros such as the BBC micro can be programmed in BASIC to carry out control and measurement tasks such as this. Our traffic lights example can be run on a small scale as a model, or the same principles can be extended to help regulate the traffic flow in a major city.

2 Robots

In science fiction stories, robots usually look something like the one in the picture opposite: mechanical machines, sometimes more intelligent than humans, able to walk, talk and reason.

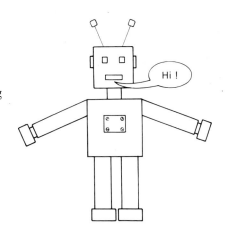

Robots in real life are very different – at least in the 1980's. They are automatic machines, programmed to perform particular tasks. Below is a picture of one kind.

This is a small industrial robot. Robots such as this one can be controlled by computer programs which send information to their servo motors. These motors are able to move the robot in various directions and operate the mechanism which makes it grasp things.

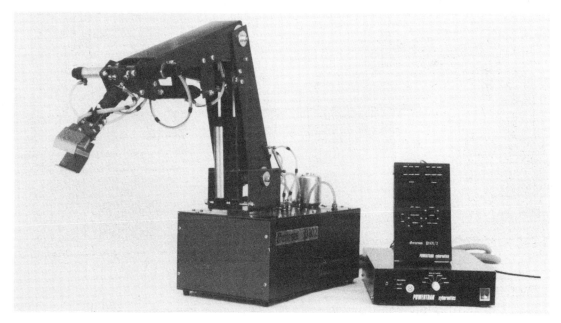

Powertran robot arm

The robot in the picture can be controlled either by its own microprocessor, which is programmed by a set of simple commands, or by linking it to the BBC micro and writing a program in BASIC. The servo motors act as analogue devices, so when a signal is being sent to the device a conversion from digital to analogue electronic information has to take place.

3 Sound and picture show

Computers can be linked to slide projectors and cassette play-back facilities to run them together automatically. They can also be used to control disco lights, as shown here.

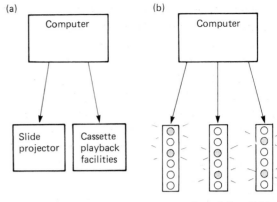

Sets of disco lights

In both cases the computer is sending digital information to digital devices.

Sound and light system

4 Measuring with the computer
Computers can be linked to many
different kinds of measuring devices.
Generally, these devices are analogue.

Look at the photograph below. It shows
a heart patient linked up to computer
controlled monitoring equipment. When
computers are used to receive information
about a patient's blood pressure or to
detect radiation, this involves constant
checking of analogue signals.

Computers can accept analogue signals
from light-sensitive cells or electrical
measuring devices. A computer can be
used as a *voltmeter* or *ammeter*,
measuring units of force or current
strength by using an analogue electrical
signal as input and converting it via a
program which displays the number on the
screen. This is useful in many areas of
industry, particularly engineering.

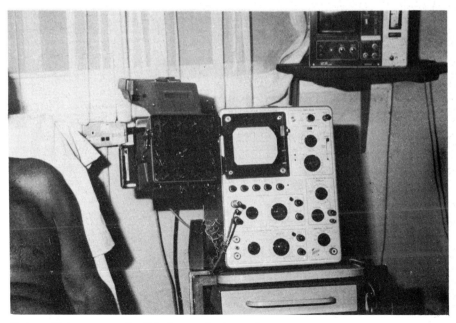

Patient with heart pacemaker linked to monitoring equipment

5 The BBC Buggy

The photograph below shows the 'BBC Buggy' – a three-wheeled vehicle which can be controlled by the BBC microcomputer. It is interesting because it combines computer control and computer measurement in one machine.

Let's look at some of the features of the BBC Buggy:

a) Control
The Buggy is powered by a pair of *stepping motors* which the computer controls to direct its movements.

b) Light-sensitivity
The Buggy is equipped with a *light sensor*. This measures light and feeds the information about it back to the machine. Because of this, the Buggy is able to follow light signals.

c) Touch-sensitivity
The Buggy is also equipped with *touch sensors*, which means that it can be programmed to find its way around objects.

d) Bar codes
The Buggy has a bar code reader attached for feeding information from

BBC Buggy in operation

bar codes back to the controlling computer. This makes it possible for the Buggy to be programmed to perform certain tasks on reading particular bar codes.

e) Graphics

The Buggy has an electromagnetically controlled pen. The computer can be programmed in a special language called LOGO to allow the Buggy to draw on a flat surface, using the pen.

4 Computers in industry

Now that we've looked at some of the computer's abilities to control and measure, and seen examples of how the BBC micro can be used for this, let's turn our attention to the use of computers in industry.

Industry is about manufacturing goods. If you live in a town, there's probably an industrial estate somewhere near you. It will contain factories with storage depots, lorry parks and, loading bays. Everything in it will be concerned with turning raw materials into a finished product that can be sold for a profit.

There are three different stages to the manufacturing process. First, the design stage: then the actual manufacturing, and finally the quality inspection. Let's look at each of these in turn.

a) Design

Before a product can be made, it has to be designed, or planned. In the case of MUSICUBE, for example, draughtsmen

and draughtswomen will have had to design the cassette box and the stages of preparing it and putting it together.

b) Manufacture

This is the actual making of the product: producing the individual pieces, and then assembling them to make the finished item.

c) Inspection

The product will need to be checked to make sure that nothing has gone wrong during manufacture and that it is of a good enough standard to sell.

We have already looked at ways in which combining computer control and measuring devices with the right hardware and software can give us machines and devices for performing many useful tasks. So far, we have been concentrating on fairly cheap devices which can be linked to the BBC micro. However the ideas behind these devices work as well on a large scale, in the factory, as they do on a small scale in the classroom. Let's look at the different stages of the manufacturing process to see how this works.

Computer-Aided Design (CAD)

Using computers to help in the design process is now such a common thing that there is a special set of letters to describe it: CAD.

CAD is useful because it saves time. An engineer or draughtsperson producing a design will usually have to make very many drawings and models. Using a computer to help, he or she can cut out many of the most time-consuming stages of the work.

In the last chapter, we looked at computer graphics. Let's see how they can help the designer. The car opposite is a good example.

When a new car comes onto the market, have you ever stopped to think how much work went into the initial design? Well, it's a great deal. Until recently, the drawings which are needed had to be produced by hand. Now, however, they can be done using CAD; that is, using computer graphics. The pictures can be input to the computer using the kind of graphics facilities we looked at in the last chapter, stored, and called up again when they are needed. This speeds up the design process considerably.

The possibilities don't end there. Computers can also help designers by actually testing out their designs, simulating the conditions in which the product will finally be used. One example of this is in the aircraft industry – when part of a new plane is being designed, computer programs are able to simulate the stresses and strains which that part would have to be able to take, and see how it would react to them.

Computer-Aided Manufacture (CAM)
Computers are becoming useful in the process of manufacturing goods. There are many ways in which they can do this. Let's look at just two of the common methods:

a) Industrial robots
We've already looked at a small example of one of these: the POWERTRAN robot. Larger and more powerful versions of robots such as this one can be programmed to perform simple tasks on a production line – spraying paint, for instance, welding parts together, or (a more difficult task) recognizing and picking up a certain type of metal part.

b) Control of industrial processes
The ability of computer systems to control processes means that they can be used to monitor industrial processes and take corrective action when necessary. In the brewing industry, for example, large tanks of liquid are given a variety of different treatments. They are constantly being checked on to see that processing is going correctly and to find out whether they are yet ready for the next stage. Computers are often used as a way of controlling this type of process. In the same way, many processes in the chemical industry can be made more efficient by using a computer system to assist with monitoring and controlling.

Inspection and testing
In processes such as the one described above, where a computer is continually monitoring what goes on, testing is taking place all the time – testing of temperature, of pressures, of other factors – and corrective action is being taken. There are also ways in which computer systems can help with checking a finished product. In the car industry, for example, it is possible to use a computer to test plastic components for the proper thickness, or to control checks on a vehicle's electrical systems.

Let's end this chapter by looking at another industry – the fashion industry – and how it can be helped by computer-aided design and manufacture. A fashion designer spends a great deal of time sketching out new fashion ideas, such as those shown on page 104.

Austin Maestro 1.3 HLE

The Maestro Body Production Line is equipped with 14 robots capable of welding five different body types

Using CAD/CAM techniques, a designer can sketch out a new idea in pattern form on a graphics tablet or digitiser. This can be fed back into the computer and stored on a device such as a floppy disc.

The design stored on the disc can then be used to direct a computer-controlled cutting machine, which can cut out the material according to the pattern. The computer program is able to produce the program for a range of sizes. Software to do this can be provided by a special package for the fashion industry.

This kind of linking together of computer graphics and control facilities is becoming increasingly common in industry. Here are some more examples of uses for the technique:

the design and testing of electronic circuits;
the design and manufacture of mechanical engineering components;
designing and producing shoes;
the design and manufacture of textiles and wallpapers.

Things to do

1 Name *three* factories to be found in your nearest large town, and describe the goods which they manufacture.

2 What are the *three* stages involved in the manufacturing of goods in an industrial concern?

3 The British Leyland factory which makes the Maestro is heavily computerised. Suggest *four* ways in which computers may be helping with the design and production of the cars.

4 What do the initials CAD and CAM stand for?

5 List *three* types of industry (other than the car industry) which you think use computers, and explain what jobs the computers do.

8

Computers and jobs

What will this chapter teach you?
This chapter explores the effects which computers are having on jobs. You'll be doing the following:

1 **looking at** a variety of jobs involving computers, the kind of people who do them, and the work which is involved;

2 **considering** how computers are affecting the job market and looking at ways to help safeguard jobs.

---

1 Computers and jobs

If you were free to pick any job you liked, what would you choose to do? Would you be an artist? A rock star? Secretary to someone important? A racing driver? An engineer? Or even a computer programmer?

Whatever you would like to do – whether it's a dream, a real ambition, or even the job you're in now – it's likely that the job of your choice involves a computer somewhere. It could be simply that your pay slip would be printed by a computer, or that you would clock in to a microcomputer when you started work; on the other hand, your chosen job might make heavy use of a computer's services. The important thing is that a great many people now use a computer in one way or another when they are at work.

Here's a list of jobs. Can you suggest where and how the people doing them

might come into contact with computers? (Write down the answers *in your work book*.) Most of them have already been mentioned in previous chapters.

1 Payroll clerk
2 Typist
3 Supermarket checkout girl
4 Airline pilot
5 Car designer
6 Cartoon animator
7 Garage mechanic
8 Teacher
9 Travel agent

There is no doubt that computers are having an effect on a large number of jobs. The result of this is that the nature of work is slowly altering. Some types of jobs are disappearing; new types of job are being created by computer technology; and a great many jobs are changing in nature. Before we try to decide what all this will mean for the future, let's look at a few of the jobs concerned. The following section deals with eight jobs involving computers, and the people doing them. These jobs have been selected to tie in with some of the applications of computers looked at in previous chapters, but they are only samples of the very many types of job which are affected.

A   The computer operator

Amina is nineteen. She is a computer operator who works in the Midlands for the head office of a chain of Do-It-Yourself stores. The company runs a number of computer systems, which have to deal with a large volume of data. To do this, it uses a main-frame computer.

Amina works in the computer room. She is one of a small team of operators who are responsible for running work on the computer. She and the other operators answer to the shift leader, who organizes the work among the shift.

The job means that Amina has to work $8\frac{1}{2}$ hour shifts, at a different time of the day every week. At first she found that the night shifts were a strain – she wasn't used to being awake at that time. After a while, however, she got used to shift work and found that there are compensations. When she's on the night shift, for example, she can visit the shops during the day; and she is paid a shift allowance on top of her basic salary.

The work itself seemed hard at first, but once she had been doing it for a while she found that it wasn't very difficult. Like anything else, it was just a matter of practice. She and the other operators have to keep the computer working at processing the company's data. This means loading programs into memory, running them, supplying the computer

with the tapes and discs that it needs, logging the shift's workload, feeding in data on cards and tapes, checking the output from the computer, watching for any error messages, and other jobs like this. Quite a lot of time is spent simply keeping the printers supplied with paper. Amina has to move heavy boxes of stationery.

Amina was lucky she got this job without any training or formal qualifications. She'd been working in one of the stores filling shelves up from the time she left school. Then, at eighteen, she applied to be a trainee computer operator. The company wasn't sure at first whether the job would suit her, but she was able to convince them that she was interested in computers and had been trying to find out about them in her spare time, so they agreed to give her a try. When she started, she found it all very new and strange, but once she'd picked it up she was promoted to be a full operator.

She likes the job. It keeps her busy and interested, and it's well paid. She's earning more than her friends who work in offices and shops. Recently, however, she's noticed that quite a few of the trainees who have joined since she did have some kind of qualification: O-level computer studies, perhaps, or a TOPS course in computer operations. Amina is keen to become a shift leader one day, and doesn't want to lose her chance to one of the newcomers, so she has started following a correspondence course to try to get some kind of qualification herself.

B   The database administrator

Charles is thirty-three. He is a database administrator working for a large company which makes biscuits. He is part of the Data Processing Department, working directly under the DP manager.

A variety of the company's systems have been combined on the computer into a database, providing quick and easy access for staff and management to information about areas such as sales, stock, products, marketing and finance. It is Charles's responsibility to organize and run this database efficently for other staff to use. He has to do the following jobs:

a) being available to consult with users of the database (ie company staff and management) and to answer enquiries;

b) overseeing the way in which the database functions;

c) monitoring the performance of the database, and adjusting it as required;

d) looking at what the users need and trying to make sure that they can get it from the database system;

e) explaining to programmers any changes needed and checking that they are made correctly.

Charles did not begin his career in the computing profession, he originally qualified in Business Studies and joined the company to do operational research. This, however, brought him into contact with the computing side, and he decided that he would like to know more. The company allowed to take a year off in order to gain an MSc in computer science; he then took a cut in salary in order to become a trainee systems analyst. This paid off, since he was rapidly promoted. He hopes that his current position will eventually lead to the offer of a management post in one of the departments that he deals with.

C   The clerk

Mike is twenty. He is an accounts clerk, part of the sales department of a large department store. He works in the accounts department, which is on the top floor. Mike's particular responsibility is looking after customers' accounts. He and the other clerks answer to the accounts manager.

Mike works at a counter separated from the customers by a glass panel, in the same way as a bank clerk. Customers come to him when they want to do business on their store account. Mike has to deal with the following things:

a) opening accounts for new customers;

b) making any changes necessary to details of accounts; for example, a customer may move and need address details changing on the records;

c) accepting payments of accounts from customers;

d) making refunds to customers;

e) answering any enquiry that a customer may make about his account;

f) closing down accounts.

Mike's job is a demanding one and he has to understand how the accounts work and also get on well with the customers. He also needs to know something about computers. This is for two reasons. One is that all the forms which he fills in when he is doing business with the customer are then passed on to a computer section, where the details are entered to the computer via VDU'S and used to alter customer records. The second is that Mike has his own VDU beside him which is directly on-line to the computer. He uses this to make enquiries for customers; for instance, to find out how much money they currently owe. Customers of the store find this service very useful to them.

Mike trained for this work by attending his local technical college for two years after leaving school and taking a qualification in business studies. This involved doing some computing, which he has since found useful. His employers continued his training when he joined them. Mike would like to learn more about the accounting work and eventually take more responsibility for the running of his section. He is only interested in the computing side of it if he can see how computers can help him to be more efficient and to give a better service to the customers.

D   The designer

Geoff is forty. He is a designer working for a company that manufactures hi-fi equipment. His job is designing cases to hold the different electronic components which together make up devices such as record decks or cassette recorders.

Geoff works in the company's design office, where he is one of several designers working under the head of the design department.

When a new hi-fi case needs designing, two important sets of factors have to be taken into account. The first set is technical, the case has to be able to hold all the components, stand up to certain heat levels, allow for certain types of connections to be made, and so on. The second set is to do with selling the finished product, the case has to be attractive to look at and match up with other products which the company sells.

A few years ago, Geoff's designs for cases were all done on paper, followed by a period of putting together mock-ups and prototypes to present each design and test it out. Now, however, Geoff uses a minicomputer to help him instead. He designs new cases at a graphics terminal, entering details of what he wants and seeing them displayed on a screen. This has several advantages. First of all, the computer already holds stored details of all the various devices which he will need to use or take into account in his design – knobs, switches, wires and so on – which means that he can call them up and add them into the blueprint which he is building up. Next, he is able to use special CAD software to run certain tests on the 'model' of the case which he has built up within the computer. He can also get a variety of different pictures of the proposed case printed out, which he is then able to present for approval or disapproval. If it should turn out to be disapproval, it is very easy for him to go back and change the details stored on the computer as needed.

Geoff trained for this job by taking an engineering degree and then joining the firm as a trainee in the design department. He is now a senior designer, and enjoys his work, particularly since he has had the computer graphics to help him. He does not wish to be promoted any higher in the company, since this would mean more administrative work and he feels that he is more at home at the technical level.

E   The programmer

Manju is twenty-two. She is a computer programmer working at the headquarters of local government offices on the south coast. Several types of computer are used there; not just a main-frame, for running large jobs, but a mini and half-a-dozen micros.

Manju works in an office as part of a project team. She is one of several programmers and analysts under the control of a project manager.

She works a $37\frac{1}{2}$ hour week normally, although sometimes she may be asked to stay on a little longer if there is a crisis or the project is running late. Her job is mainly concerned with writing and testing computer programs. It works like this:

a) One of the analysts gives her a PROGRAM SPECIFICATION; that is, a description of the program she has to write and what it needs to do.

b) Manju reads the specification, talks to the analyst, and designs and flowcharts the program.

c) She writes the program in a computer language. For most of the programs she writes for the main-frame, that will be COBOL, a business-orientated language. Recently, however, she has been writing some BASIC programs to run on the microcomputers.

d) She inputs the program to the computer by typing it in, or by having it punched onto cards and then read in by a card reader.

e) She tests that the program works by running it many times with different data.

Manju sometimes does other things as well; for instance, making changes to existing programs, or helping to write program specifications.

Manju has six O-levels and an A-level in computer science; she is now working in the evenings and on day release to gain an HNC in computer studies. Most of the other programmers have similar qualifications; some have degrees. She joined the organization straight from school, after having taken an aptitude test for programming computers.

Manju enjoys the work, although when she has a particularly obstinate fault in one of the programs she sometimes finds that her temper is wearing a bit thin! At the moment, she is trying to decide what she wants to do in the future – whether it's best to stay as a programmer but gaining more experience and becoming fluent in many computer languages, or whether to move further away from the technical side and find out more about what her programs are being used for.

F   The analyst

Alan is twenty-seven. He is a systems analyst working for local government, on the same project team as Manju. Like Manju he has a basic week of $37\frac{1}{2}$ hours, although he also sometimes has to work longer hours.

Alan's job is partly technical and partly to do with the people who use computer systems. It works like this:

a) A new computer system is needed – perhaps a financial one, to analyse budget figures for the County Treasurer. The project manager puts Alan in charge of the new work.

b) Alan talks at length with the Treasurer and the staff who need the system, to find out exactly what they want and how they will be using it. He looks at their current system, to decide how it can best be improved.

c) Alan writes a first description of what the new system should do, and agrees this with the staff who are to be the users.

d) Alan produces a technical design for the system, including program specifications. These are passed out to programmers, who then write and test the programs needed.

e) Alan does further testing on the programs which make up the new system, and trains operators in how to run it and users in how to use it.

f) The system 'goes live'.

Alan's job isn't always as clearcut as this; like Manju, his work involves all kinds of different activities.

Alan needed quite a lot of qualifications to get this job. He has a degree in Business Studies, which helps him with the user side of his work; his technical experience came from three years as a programmer, during which time his employers sent him on several courses. He is currently studying to gain a professional qualification.

Not all the analysts had this kind of background. Sara, the other analyst on Alan's project team, took an HNC in computer studies, but she joined the local government headquarters to work in the administration at first. After some years in this area of work, it seemed natural that she should combine the two things by becoming a trainee systems analyst.

Alan's ambition is to become first a senior analyst, doing the more responsible jobs, and then to become a project manager in charge of a whole team.

G The typist

Louise is twenty. She is a shorthand typist working in the typing pool of a large London firm of accountants. She and the other typists are responsible to the office manager, who also schedules their work.

Louise has to type all kinds of different documents, from letters to complicated reports. Sometimes she is called to take dictation from one of the accountants in the firm and then has to type it up from her shorthand notes; at other times, she works as an audio-typist, typing directly from dictation which has been recorded beforehand.

Louise was seventeen when she first came to work for the firm, after having successfully completed a course in shorthand and typing at her local technical college. In those days, the firm used electric typewriters, of the kind Louise had learned to use as part of her training.

A year ago, however, there was a change in Louise's job. The company that she works for decided to install word processors to replace the typewriters. Not only were new machines brought in, but Louise and the other typists had to be sent on a special training course to teach them how to operate them.

At first, Louise was worried about the changeover. She had been using a typewriter for some years now, was happy with it, and knew that she could do her job well. There was no guarantee, though, that she would get on with a computer. Louise had never had anything to do with computers, and she wasn't sure that she could cope with one. Worst of all, there was a rumour going round that the new machines were so good that they would do away with the need for human typists entirely!

There was no help for it however, it had all been agreed between the unions and the management and the new machines would be used. So Louise took the course, and by the end of it, she felt reassured. It wasn't so difficult to operate a word processor after all; in fact once she had got over her first fear of them she had liked the machines. Also, it was clear that people were still as important as ever.

Her job was safe.

Louise is still a shorthand typist, but she uses a word processor these days rather than a typewriter. Now that she has been working on one for quite a while, she finds that it makes her job quicker and easier. This has also meant a productivity bonus for all the staff in the typing pool, which means that Louise now earns more money for the same working hours. She is hoping to become a secretary soon, but would still like to keep her word processor rather than go back to a typewriter.

2 Computers and employment

The effects of computers on our lives are not all good. One of the most worrying is that they can put people out of jobs. There is no doubt that this is happening. Most at risk are semi-skilled and clerical occupations – things like filing, processing paperwork and some factory work can be done efficiently by computer. Losing a job is never pleasant, and at time when general unemployment is high it can be disastrous for many people.

However, the picture isn't all gloomy. New jobs are also created. We've already looked at some of these – programmers, operators and analysts are all occupations which haven't been around for very long, for example. Then there are the engineers who service the machines, the clerks who enter and check the data, and many others.

During a time of economic depression, it's difficult to assess accurately the position of computers and jobs. Assuming, however, that some jobs *are* under threat, what can be done about it? We can't put back the clock; computers are with us, and will need to stay with us if we are to remain competitive in our business and industry. That doesn't mean, however, that we can ignore the problem and hope that it will go away. There are several groups of people who have a role to play:

a) *Managers*
   The people who take the decision to bring computers into their organizations have a responsibility to their staff to see that as little disruption as possible is caused and that the human implications of the new technology are given a lot of thought.

b) *The unions*
   These have a responsibility to represent their members and keep a watchful eye on the effects of any computers which are being introduced. This is often done by means of a 'new technology' agreement, which safeguards the interests of the people in the organization.

c) *The computer staff*
   These need to think of the computer systems which they are installing in terms of their effects on people, not just as machines, and to design their systems with human beings in mind.

d) *The workers*
   This means *you*. The best thing you can possibly do to help is to find out about computers, on the old principle that 'if you can't beat them, join them!' We're not saying that you need to become a computer expert – there are plenty of them around already – you need to do just what you're already doing: to find out what the machines can do and become confident in using one. That way, if a computer system is installed in *your* factory or office, you'll be right there knowing about it and ready to use it to help you do your job. That's what being computer literate is all about.

Things to do

1 Copy and complete the table *in your workbook* by connecting lines to show which of the eight people described in this chapter you would expect to find doing each of the activities below:

Feeding data on punched cards into a computer	THE COMPUTER OPERATOR
	THE DATABASE ADMINISTRATOR
Using a word processor	THE CLERK
Talking to users about how they want their central collection of data organised	THE DESIGNER
Writing the technical design for a computer system	THE PROGRAMMER
Drawing a flowchart of a program's logic	
Enquiring through a VDU to find out about a customer's account	THE ANALYST
Using a computer simulation to test a new design	THE TYPIST

2 Decide which of the seven jobs described in this chapter most appeals to you, and make a plan of the actions – educational or otherwise – you would need to take if you wanted to follow up this interest.

Into the future!

So you've done it. You've read this book from cover to cover, digested the contents, and completed all the activities recommended in it. You've also had your hands on a computer and you are now fully confident in how to handle it and get the program you need loaded-in and running. You can talk about software, hardware and microprocessors with the best of them. You are, in fact, officially Computer Literate. Now what?

Unfortunately, *one* of you isn't enough. We need a whole nation of people like you – people who are at home with computers – and we need them fast, because everything to do with computers is moving at breakneck speed. It's often said that the rate of change is so rapid that we're going through an Information Technology Revolution. Certainly, you've only got to look through the colour supplements or browse through the High Street stores to realize that computers are moving into everyday life. If you go further and glance through any of the many specialist and hobby magazines about computers to be found in almost any newsagent, you'll be dazzled by the sheer range of different types of hardware and software to be found. There's an explosion of ideas, materials and equipment going on.

Let's look at how all this might affect just one citizen – a person picked out of a hat and watched as she goes about her daily affairs in our new Information

Technology World. We'll call her Linda Bould. She's a businesswoman involved in the manufacture of fashion garments. Let's track her progress through a day's activities.

7.00 am   The alarm goes off. It's microprocessor-controlled, of course. As Linda Bould struggles to wake up, her morning tea arrives – both made and brought by a robot which is a smaller domestic version of the individual ones we have already seen.

8.00 am   Breakfast. She has cornflakes and an egg. Because she is computer literate, she knows that the milk she uses comes from a cow whose milk yield has been electronically monitored and whose feed has been adjusted accordingly; that the cereal has also been through a computer-monitored process; and that the egg came from a chicken whose environment was controlled by yet more computer technology. It must be admitted, however, that Linda doesn't think about any of this at eight in the morning!

8.20 am   Post and mail. Are there any bills? Have any friends written? What's the weather forecast for the day? What are the national headlines? To answer these, and other questions like them, she doesn't have to wait for the post or newspaper – she goes straight to the VDU to see if there is any electronic mail in the computer 'in-tray'. She finds a letter from her mother and a bill. Quickly, she types in a reply to send to her mother, but decides to wait a week before giving the command to pay the bill from the bank account. That taken care of, she is able to spend a few moments looking through the news on the public databank service.

9.05 am   A business meeting. She is still at home. Sitting at the work-desk, she is able to call up her colleagues by typing in a command at the keyboard. This gives her a telephone link with each of them, a televised picture of them, and all the data needed for the meeting.

11.30 am   Another business meeting, this time with a colleague who isn't yet fully computerised. She doesn't mind; it makes a pleasant trip. She walks to the nearest station and uses her plastic identity card to give her access to the platform. The train she takes is driverless, controlled completely by computer; automatic sensors make sure that it doesn't come dangerously near to any other trains.

1.00 am   Lunch. Linda and colleague go to an I. T. FAST FOOD restaurant. She feeds her plastic card into a terminal and then keys in her selection. The food is delivered by another robot, and the cost is automatically deducted from her bank account.

2.00 am   Visit to the factory. Her plastic card, fed into the factory terminal, passes her through the security checks, and she is able to see the work of the factory going on. Lasers, linked to robots, are cutting out clothes of various sizes and patterns. The factory makes clothes to measure for customers who send their requirements from on-line terminals in shops. Keying into a VDU, Linda does a spot check on quality and production rate; then, well satisfied, sets off for home. On the way, she notices a blind person waiting at a bus stop, and is not surprised when the person knows of the arrival of the right number bus by using an electronic receiver to pick up the signal from the bus.

6.30 pm Time to relax. Since it is a fine summer evening, Linda takes her microcomputer into the hills and uses it to 'paint' a landscape, using graphics facilities. Returning home, she has a copy of the picture printed out.

Still in a creative mood, she uses her microcomputer to compose a tune, takes a copy and plays it happily on the piano for a while.

There is time then for a quick round of computer golf, and then electronically mailing a letter to a friend.

11.30 pm Daily medical checkup. Linda attaches sensors to her body to record her heart and blood pressure. These are then automatically transmitted to her doctor's medical files on disc. And so to bed. . . .

Could this ever be you? The thought of a day like this can be either attractive or horrifying. It may all seem very far in the future, and yet there's nothing in this story which couldn't, in theory, happen now.

The technology is *already with us*. What we have to decide is how to use it, what kind of lives we want to live, both now and in the future. Will our new world provide more time for leisure, giving everyone the chance to enjoy countryside and culture, to follow up their own talents and interests? Will it mean that there aren't enough jobs to go round? Will it lead to less contact with other people, so that we all live lives which are increasingly private? Or, on the other hand, will it mean that all the details about us are held on public files which anyone can get at and there will be no privacy at all? Will it spell out the end for boring jobs? Will it lead to increased prosperity for everyone?

These are the kinds of questions which are being asked. Now that you are computer literate, you too should be able to think about these issues and play your part in trying to ensure that the new technology enriches our lives rather than impoverishing them.

Glossary

(This glossary defines the main computer vocabulary used during the book, in non-specialist terms rather than by giving detailed technical definitions.)

Analogue Operating on a principle of continuous variance (see Digital)
Application Any use to which a computer is put

Backing storage Any form of storage which a computer uses to keep information which is not permanently held in memory – tape and disc are commonly used types
Bar code A strip containing lines of different widths representing information which can be read directly into a computer
BASIC The language most commonly used on microcomputers
Batch processing A type of computer processing where data is dealt with a group at a time

CAD Computer-Aided Design – the use of computer facilities such as graphics to assist designers
CAM Computer-Aided Manufacture – the use of computer facilities to control or assist in the manufacturing process. Often linked with CAD
COBOL A business-orientated computer language which is widely used in commercial organizations
Computer An electronic machine which processes data automatically
CPU Central Processing Unit – the 'brain' of the computer which controls processing.
Cursor The small bar which shows the user his or her position on a VDU screen

Data Words, numbers, pictures or other information handled by a computer
Databank An organized collection of information held on a computer which is available to the public through computer terminals
Database An organized collection of information held on a computer
Data processing Handling raw data to produce useful information (usually by computer)
Digital Operating by use of 'stepped' numbers (see Analogue)
Direct access Obtaining a piece of information directly from computer storage without needing to go through intervening data

File A structure for storing linked items of information
Floppy disc A method of backing storage, commonly used with small computer systems
Flowchart A diagrammatic method of illustrating a logical sequence of events or flow of data
FORTRAN A scientifically-orientated computer language in common use in scientific and engineering applications

Graphics Computer handling of pictures and diagrams

Hard disc A high-volume method of backing storage
Hardware The physical equipment making up a computer system

Information technology The storage, manipulation and transmission of any form of data, using computers and communications facilities
Input How data gets into a computer system

Interface   The boundary or connecting device between two parts of a computer system

Language   A set of rules for giving a computer instructions
LOGO   An educational computer language based around the use of graphics

Main-frame   The largest size of computer, characterized by relatively high cost, storage capacity and processing power
Memory   A form of storage which is immediately available to a computer and in which all processing is done
Microchip/silicon chip   A device containing microelectronic circuits on a slice of silicon
Microcomputer   The smallest, 'desk-top' size of computer
Microprocessor   A silicon chip containing a control and processing unit
Minicomputer   The size of computer falling between 'mainframes' and 'micros'

On-line processing   Sending data to and from a computer down a communication line

Package   Standard ready-written software suitable for more than one user
Peripheral   Any device connected to the central processing unit of a computer
Program   A set of instructions telling a computer what to do

Real-time processing   On-line processing

where details held on a computer are altered almost at once
Robot   A device which is equipped with sensors and mechanical parts and which is computer or microprocessor controlled

Sensor   A device for detecting and registering physical signals
Serial access   A method of obtaining information from computer storage which requires going through intervening data first
Silicon chip   See Microchip
Simulation   Use of a computer to build internal models
Systems analyst   Someone who specializes in analysing a systems problem and suggesting or designing a solution which usually involves the use of a computer

Teletext   A service which uses the television signal to send requested information to a TV screen eg ORACLE, CEEFAX
Terminal   A device which is on-line to a computer

Validation   Checking input data for errors
Variable   A labelled program area in which values can be stored
Viewdata   A databank service which uses telephone lines to send and receive information eg PRESTEL

Word processor   A computer with devices and programs specially designed for handling text

Index

office machines, 63–76
office staff, 60–3
off-the-shelf software, 77, 90
on-line processing, 84–90, 91, 107
operator, 106, 110, 111, 112
ORACLE, 89–90
order processing system, 74–5
output, 3–7, 21, 49, 52, 69, 95, 96–7

package, 90
paper-tape, 11
payroll system, 72–4, 76
peripherals, 10, 17
photocopiers, 65
PRESTEL, 88–90
printer, 15–16
processor, 4–6, 8, 10, 17, 49
program, 8–10, 20, 26–8, 29–43, 57, 69, 70, 72, 74–6, 77–91, 97, 104, 109–10, 112
program specification, 109–10
programmer, 108–9, 111, 112
punched cards, 11, 84–5, 109, 112

real-time processing, 85–7
robot, 97–8, 102, 113

sensors, 100, 113, 114
serial access, 69
silicon chip, 2, 45, 51
simulation, 79–81, 82, 102, 112
software, 9, 51, 75, 77, 90, 104, 112
systems analyst, 109–10, 111, 112

teletext, 89–90
teletypewriter, 12
telex, 67
transistor, 2, 49–50, 53
typewriters, 63–4, 67, 71–2, 110–11
typist, 110–11, 112

validation, 84–7
valves, 47–50, 53
variables, 36–8, 42
Viewdata, 88–90
visual display unit (VDU), 8, 10, 16, 41, 74, 78, 84, 85, 88, 107, 112, 113, 114

word processor, 71–3, 76, 92, 110–11, 112